Nevada's Environmental Legacy

T0288212

Wilbur S. Shepperson Series in Nevada History

Nevada's Environmental Legacy

PROGRESS OR PLUNDER

James W. Hulse

University of Nevada Press

RENO & LAS VEGAS

Wilbur S. Shepperson Series in Nevada History
Series Editor: Michael Green
University of Nevada Press, Reno, Nevada 89557 USA
Copyright © 2009 by University of Nevada Press
All rights reserved
Manufactured in the United States of America
Design by Kathleen Szawiola

Library of Congress Cataloging-in-Publication Data
Hulse, James W.
Nevada's environmental legacy : progress or plunder /
James W. Hulse.
p. cm. — (Wilbur S. Shepperson series in Nevada history)
Includes bibliographical references and index.
ISBN 978-0-87417-769-5 (pbk. : alk. paper)
1. Nevada—Environmental conditions. 2. Environmental policy—
Nevada—History. 3. Natural resources—Nevada—History.
4. Nature—Effect of human beings on—Nevada—History.
5. Environmental degradation—Nevada—History. I. Title.
GE155.N3H85 2009
333.709793—dc22   2008041467

The paper used in this book is a recycled stock made from 30 percent
post-consumer waste materials, certified by FSC, and meets the
requirements of American National Standard for Information
Sciences—Permanence of Paper for Printed Library Materials,
ANSI/NISO Z39.48-1992 (R2002). Binding materials were selected for
strength and durability.

FIRST PRINTING
18 17 16 15 14 13 12 11 10 09
5 4 3 2 1

For our Grandchildren,
Who will Harvest
What We Planted

Aboveground nuclear explosion, Nevada Test Site, 1950s
Carl Sagan at antinuclear-test protest, near Nevada Test Site
Tunnel portal, Yucca Mountain
Reno from the air, looking west
Restoring the Truckee River channel

MAPS

Have we citizens of Nevada been snoozing while the exploiters and profiteers have been taking over our homestead? This is a crude rhetorical question about what has been happening to Nevada in the recent past. It invites more serious public debate on environmental issues.

In this book I offer an assessment of Nevada's environmental experience over the past 150 years. Within the lifetime of some of our senior citizens, we have witnessed profound changes in the natural environment of the state and in our attitudes toward these changes. We have witnessed urban sprawl, a revolution in mining and smelting techniques, transformations of the rangelands, an expanded military presence, development of the Atomic Test Site, the M-X fiasco, a presidential decision to place a national nuclear waste depository in Nevada, and a proposal to make a massive water transfer from rural eastern Nevada to the Las Vegas Valley— among other challenging events. My intention is to discuss these developments within the broader perspective of Nevada history.

One of the most daunting problems facing our contemporary world, including Nevada, is the pollution and degradation of the environment. So far, historians writing on Nevada have said too little on this subject, and we have made little use of the most obvious evidence before us. I offer this document as a corrective, especially to my own writings but also to others. This book has few answers to the many questions about Nevada's environment that have arisen in recent decades, but my hope is that it will promote further serious inquiry and deeper investigation into the pressing issues.

Environmental concerns have been on the margins of books about Nevada from the beginning of the state's history. Most early writings focused on extracting wealth from the earth, "improving" the land, and building profitable businesses on a challenging terrain. But some of these texts gave little attention to the long-term environmental consequences of all this activity.

Subsequent writings have presented Nevada as a tourist-tempting destination, a relic of the romantic Old West, or a colorful setting in which people can escape their mundane lives within a neon-lit casino. But again, most general studies of Nevada's culture and commerce have left environmental questions on the periphery, like extras or a chorus on the fringes of the stage. This book tries to give these questions a higher billing.

Recently, there have been some scholarly studies and popular writings about the one aspect of Nevada's environmental realities that seems to concern a wide audience. However, most discussions about the Nevada Test Site and military training and testing activities are fairly limited and not especially enlightening.

A small but crucial body of writing has been produced by protestors, using their prophetic voices to sound the alarums for protection of Nevada's fragile natural heritage. Nevada has benefited from private groups like the Sierra Club, Citizen Alert, Great Basin Mine Watch, and the Progressive Leadership Alliance of Nevada (PLAN). These organizations have been the conscience of Nevada on environmental matters for many years. I have tried to draw upon this work—which represents a fairly slender body of writing and effective activism—and to glean from it wherever possible important information about threats to Nevada's environmental well-being.

Late in 2004, the U.S. Census Bureau reported that Nevada led the nation in the percentage of population increase for the eighteenth consecutive year. Most of this growth happened in the Las Vegas Valley, and some of it also along the eastern edge of the Sierra Nevada around Reno and Carson City. The southern triangle around Las Vegas is a laboratory where population explosion, a consumption-oriented economy, and ongoing technological revolution are merging in a puzzling triangulation. Whether the problems created by this situation are soluble, and if so, how they are to be solved, are matters of vital national concern as the country's population continues to grow and continues to shift into the arid, environmentally fragile West.

The rest of the state—90 percent of its territory—has endured less population pressure than the swelling urban centers, but the environmental problems arising there from other causes are among the most profound and most worrisome in the nation. The impacts of overgrazing, massive mining operations, military testing, and water transfer to urban centers may, if not addressed, prove catastrophic.

This book is a chronicle about attracting, tempting, and seducing Nevadans, not only by those who came to exploit, make money, and explode their arsenal on this turf, but also by those who have loved the state. The text that follows is about the uses and abuses of Nevada's land, water, and air, and about the efforts of those who have tried to build the commonwealth and mitigate the damage created by their own efforts or those of their predecessors.

M y intellectual debts as a historian grow larger every year. Nevada scholars and friends whom I have often acknowledged in the past are high on my list. The scholarly legacies of Russell Elliott and Wilbur Shepperson still provide useful dividends. More recent historians, especially William Rowley of the University of Nevada, Reno; Eugene Moehring and the late Hal Rothman of the University of Nevada Las Vegas; and Michael Green of the College of Southern Nevada have all offered new investments to the fund of insights. The works of Scott Slovic and Cheryll Glotfelty of the University of Nevada, Reno, English Department have also been invaluable.

Once again, librarians and archivists across the state have made this task easier. In their league also are the public information officers of the government and private agencies. Among these are Cindy Peterson, formerly of the Nevada Division of Environmental Protection; Franklin Pemberton and Ed Monnig of the U.S. Forest Service; and Jo Simpson. James Taranik, director of UNR's Mackay School of Earth Sciences and Engineering, was generous as usual with his time and assistance. My quest was empowered by the kindness of Vanya Scott of the Atomic Testing Museum in Las Vegas. Kathy War of the UNLV Library's Special Collections Department has repeatedly responded to my search for information. Glenn Miller, the senior expert of the Nevada environmental movement, read this manuscript at an early stage and was most helpful. Tina Nappe and Bob Fulkerson read it at a later stage and gave indispensable advice. Robert Loux and Joseph Strolin of the Nevada Agency for Nuclear Projects have been extremely helpful. And I thank Elizabeth Dilly of The Nature Conservancy, who played an important role in improving this text and its photographs. Its gaps or lapses belong to me.

The superb work of the Nevada Bureau of Mines and Geology has been indispensable. Kris Ann Pizarro has been generous with her skills in cartography and her photograph collection. The team at the University of Nevada Press has been my enabling mentor with this experiment as on several previous ventures. For more than forty years, they have improved my prose and possibilities.

At times Nevada has resembled Faust, the classic Germanic gambler, who made a pact with the devil—Goethe's image of the satanic tempter. Faust was assured he could enjoy all the pleasures he could imagine here and now, if only he would surrender his soul to Satan at the end of the game—when he had finally had enough. This is a rough metaphor with many flaws, but adequate for the present purposes. My role in this experiment is to ask a few Socratic questions in this Faustian situation in the hope the inquiries will invite more discussion and ethical work.

As this essay approaches its finale, our grandchildren come to mind. Wherever they are in time and space, we owe them testimony about how the planet and our little piece of it have been treated on their ancestors' watch.

Nevada's Environmental Legacy

CHAPTER ONE

Land Policies

When Nevada became a state in 1864, the U.S. government was trying to get rid of public lands as quickly as possible, in an effort to "privatize" the vast landscape of the West. Congress encouraged homesteading, railroad building, and the establishment of schools and colleges, which allowed easy transfer of land. This national giveaway policy existed for another ninety years in the Far West.

Congress tried to ensure that most acres in the West were sold in an orderly manner to citizens through government land offices; the revenue for cheap land sales would flow into federal and state treasuries. In much of the inland West, however, settlers, grazers, and miners arrived before the land officers. The exploiters who got there first took what they wanted, and often moved on.

Those who made early policy were not troubled by the ecological damage that might occur or the displacement of Native peoples. Hearty pioneers—much celebrated in American history and legend—who responded to the westward surge in the nineteenth century were even less concerned. The original farmers, ranchers, and miners who arrived in Nevada simply occupied the land and claimed it under an alodial doctrine, a little-understood principle as ancient as the migrations of peoples. Whoever took the land first and used it (as long as they were Caucasian) did not need the authority of a government to do so. Thomas Jefferson, among others, affirmed this land-use principle. Nature's gifts were among the "natural rights" of men, not a privilege to be conferred by some distant authority. If you occupied and used unclaimed land, it was yours. (Such privileges, of course, did not apply to women or minority groups in the nineteenth century.)

Land and water practices in the Far West were like a buffet table: those who arrived first took generous portions; those who came later got the scraps. Nevada's resources in particular were not well displayed: open arid spaces, undependable streams, and crude rock ledges were the most obvious features. Rich soil and luxuriant forests—abundant in the eastern United States and California— were scarce in Nevada, especially after the mining boom swept through. Early arrivals took generous portions of whatever they thought they could use and either held on or moved on if the area did not suit their appetites.

The earliest beneficiaries of the federal largesse in land were the railroads, livestock barons, and the mining fraternity. Small farmers and homesteaders, the intended beneficiaries of federal policies, lagged far behind in attaining both land and water resources in Nevada. In some cases the large livestock companies sponsored small farms, though traditional farming, as practiced in the East and Midwest, was not practical in most parts of Nevada.

The efforts by Congress and various federal agencies to dispose of Nevada's land in the nineteenth century were only marginally successful. Evolving law in the twentieth century began to regard the unclaimed public land as a national trust, to be preserved with future generations in mind (about 87 percent of the acreage remained under federal management at the beginning of 2009). Yet some segments of industry and rural society regarded this vast federal domain as their own backyard playground, to be used and abused for their private interests. Whereas in the twentieth century, some branches of the federal government generally tried to protect the land from exploiters, in the first decade of the twenty-first, during the presidency of George W. Bush, the stewardship concept was once again under siege.

The Railroad Giveaway

The drama of building the transcontinental railroad is etched deeply in the nation's memory. In the late twentieth century, many were still celebrating the driving of the golden and silver spikes at Promontory, Utah, in 1869, connecting the Far West to the center of the nation with a ribbon of iron. In 2000 Stephen E. Ambrose published his monumental history *Nothing Like It in the World: The Men Who Built the Transcontinental Railroad, 1863–1869,* providing an exhilarating renewal of the story and paying tribute to all those who constructed the great artery. The technological skills of the engineers, the promotional talents of the fund-raisers, and the sweat of the laborers created a miracle of "modern" transportation. It was the space-age accomplishment of the nineteenth century.

The Big Four of the Central Pacific oligarchy—Collis P. Huntington, Mark Hopkins, Charles Crocker, and Leland Stanford—hoodwinked the federal government and exploited the states and territories through which their railroad passed, receiving an abundant helping of northern Nevada's land resources through an act of Congress in the 1860s, even before Nevada became a state. Under the laws giving the Central Pacific the authority and incentive to build the 433 miles of roadbed across Nevada, the company received title to alternate sections of land on both sides of the main line to a width of about 10 miles, or a total of 5 million acres.

The railroad initially stimulated Nevada's economy by establishing new communities such as Reno, Winnemucca, Battle Mountain, and Elko. It provided access to the mines of the Comstock Lode after the Virginia & Truckee spur line had been built into Reno in 1872 and reduced the cost of freight shipments to and from Nevada mines and ranches. But the railroad owners also

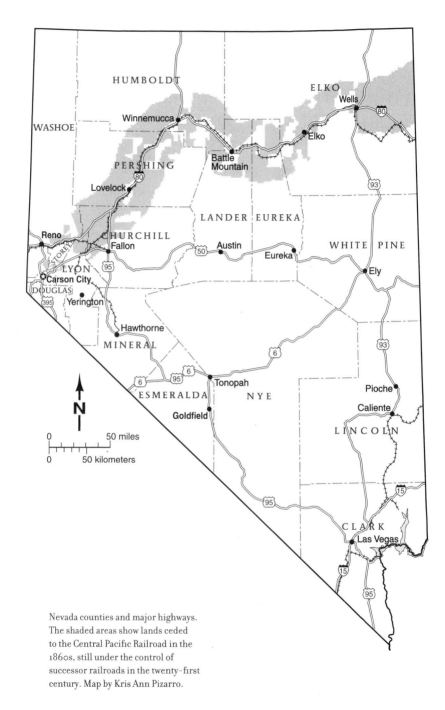

Nevada counties and major highways.
The shaded areas show lands ceded
to the Central Pacific Railroad in the
1860s, still under the control of
successor railroads in the twenty-first
century. Map by Kris Ann Pizarro.

strangled Nevada's early commercial possibilities by imposing excessive freight rates for the last three decades of the nineteenth century. In fact, the railroad was regarded throughout much of the West as a hungry leech, sucking the nourishment from the regions through which it passed.

Benefits reaped by railroad investors and promoters were much greater than any advantages that flowed to the pioneers and settlers (with the possible exception of the livestock barons). The railroad owners brought capitalist values to the construction project (with the generous help of more federal subsidies) and built the railroad through the muscle and sweat of Chinese coolies and other low-paid workers. Laying tracks through the Sierra Nevada and across the Great Basin to the Great Salt Lake was a formidable challenge; the ingenuity of the Big Four moguls and brute force of the workers were equal to it.

A century later, successor corporations to the Central Pacific sold off millions of acres and continued to profit from the well-intentioned giveaway of the 1860s. In the 1970s the discovery and development of vast quantities of microscopic gold along the Humboldt River corridor gave another windfall to the railroad owners or their heirs. This inheritance came from corporate ancestors who had acquired much of their wealth through trickery and profiteering.

The development of federal and interstate highway systems in the twentieth century was a consequence of the introduction of automobiles and trucks to the nation's transportation system. The impact of these arterials affected the rapidly growing urban areas with more travelers and more air pollution and global warming—problems that governments tried to address later with only modest success.

The Rangeland Dilemma

Another, less intentional, giveaway occurred in the earliest years of statehood. When Congress formulated land policies for the Far West after the Civil War, it responded to those who were already settling on the plains and prairies. But the government was impotent when emigrants simply occupied the space that appealed to them. The cattlemen who herded their livestock on a seasonal basis assumed land belonged to those who used it.

The cowman tending his "doggies" and the lonely sheepherder watching his flock have been raw material for folklore and literary tributes throughout the West. Cowboys and sheepherders have traditionally been regarded as western knights of virtue, symbols of the independent, hardworking American individualist. This myth—perhaps it was reality in the nineteenth century—ran into conflict with national policy in the twentieth. Too many cowmen and sheepherders had livestock on the desert terrain to allow the rangeland to renew itself. For this reason, the federal government intervened. It tried to bring justice to an unruly citizenry, and its "help" was often unwelcome.

The concept of public domain gradually changed during the century after Nevada joined the Union. Two units of the federal bureaucracy—the U.S. Forest Service and the Bureau of Land Management—began to exercise their responsibilities as trustees for more than 80 percent of the land within the state. But their agents arrived on the scene well after cattlemen, sheepherders, and miners had established themselves. When these agencies tried to enforce the standards imposed by law, they were often regarded by the local populations as intruders, even hostile foreigners.

Range management involved a challenging set of problems in the last years of the twentieth century. After decades of overgrazing and neglect, the most accessible and desirable forage for livestock had been nibbled or trampled to the edge of extinction. Native bunchgrasses were disappearing; mountain streams were being trampled into stinking gullies. This process is summarized in three thoughtful books published in the late-twentieth- and early-twenty-first centuries. Each looks at the challenge of defining land-use policy in Nevada and the Far West. Together, they encapsulate the changing attitude toward the livestock business in recent decades.

The earliest was *Cattle in the Cold Desert* (1985), by James A. Young and B. Abbott Sparks. It describes the evolution of ranching empires in the Great Basin over the past century and a half. With emphasis on the challenges faced by cattlemen before 1900, it centers on John Sparks, who ran big herds both on private land and in the public domain. This "open-range" period of livestock grazing was brief but romantic, enshrining the cowboy as an American icon. Environmental concerns associated with the commercial uses of the land were secondary.

The second book, reflecting a broader, more ecologically sensitive point of view, is by Paul F. Starrs, a University of Nevada geographer. Titled *Let the Cowboy Ride: Cattle Ranching in the American West* (1998), this volume embraces the concerns that have become more common in the recent era. With a pleasant, loping style appropriate to its theme, it resembles a well-organized cattle drive. Starrs demonstrates that the land policy inherited from the East did not serve well the practices and traditions of western livestock ranchers. The small family-size farms contemplated by the Jefferson ideal were not practical or profitable in regions such as the arid Great Basin (although hundreds of settlers gave that dream their best efforts in the late nineteenth century). The 160-acre quarter sections, neatly arranged in checkerboard fashion in places such as the Ohio River valley, were not workable in the water-starved landscape of the Far West. Instead, it was the barons of the cattle and sheep industry—not the small farmers—who dominated the agricultural business in Nevada during the first hundred years of statehood. Figures such as L. R. "Broadhorns" Bradley, Jewett Adams, and John Sparks (all of whom became governors) ran their herds in the sagebrush-covered valleys largely on federally owned land. Such men usually prospered, unless a severe winter devastated their herds. The passage of the Desert Land Act of 1877 was one in a series of laws from Congress that tried to make it easier for men and women to bring the high western terrain under the plow. Much of this legislation, as Starrs notes, "did little more than open a floodgate of fraudulent entries" (53).

A fact of life in Nevada—as in most other western states—is that the unregulated rangelands were badly overgrazed by livestock. In 1934 Congress took official notice of this undisputed fact and passed the Taylor Grazing Act, which sought to limit and regulate the number of animals allowed in each region. The law had some beneficial results; it retarded but did not stop the most destructive practices. This point brings us to the final book in our triad of rangeland studies, a challenging opus in the literature of rangeland analysis, *Welfare Ranching: The Subsidized Destruction of the American West* (2002). This volume came from a symposium assembled by George Wuerthner and Mollie Matteson and includes scores of photographs to complement a powerful indictment of abusive land-use practices and policies. For example, *Welfare Ranching* gives pictorial evidence of a little-known fact, troubling to longtime Nevadans who affectionately call their home turf "the sagebrush state": sagebrush—the state flower—can become an intruder that results from overgrazing, crowding out native grasses and natural forage that wildlife seeks.

Nevada historians have often taken note of the overgrazing of the rangelands by cattlemen, sheepherders, and, later, wild horses, but we have seldom looked at the ecological results. Large cattle herds not only eat more grass than the arid desert ecosystem can restore, but they also trample and pollute watering holes. In the delicate foothill terrain between the high mountains and the broad valleys where native wildlife naturally grazes, domesticated livestock leave little behind for antelope and deer.

A glimmer of hope existed for restoring the rangelands of northern Nevada in the early 2000s. The number of sheep and cattle in the valleys declined through most of the twentieth century. Whereas there were more than a million sheep in the 1920s and 1930s, the number had dwindled to about fifty thousand in the mid-1990s, and the number of cattle was also sharply reduced. Recurring droughts and uncertainties in the livestock markets may account for some of this transition, but it is mainly due to changing market forces. Eighty years ago, Great Basin rangeland was a friendly venue for raising livestock, because beef cattle and sheep could be fed and transported inexpensively from the high desert to distant markets. By the late twentieth century, though, this scenario had changed. Nevada learned belatedly what more heavily populated parts of the world already knew—that cattle and sheep could be raised more efficiently in tightly managed situations. This squeeze on Nevada's agricultural mainstay fueled resentment that livestock owners of northern Nevada already felt for the federal government—and especially for the Bureau of Land Management. The Taylor Grazing Act of 1934 had annoyed many, and its most emphatic sequel—the Federal Land Policy Management Act (FLPMA) of 1976—came to cowboy country of northern Nevada as a slap in the face.

In enacting FLPMA (sometimes called "Flip Ma"), Congress provided that most of the public domain would remain under control of the national government permanently, with few exceptions. The giveaway era had ended, and those resources that remained would now be managed or distributed according to plan. It was prudent policy for a nation that had been wasteful of its resources for two hundred years and had grown to more than 250 million people.

FLPMA provoked the "Sagebrush Rebellion," which originated in Elko County. Cattlemen and their allies in northeastern Nevada led the movement that prompted the 1979 session of the Nevada legislature to lay claim to millions of acres—more than half the state—which were under the control of the Bureau of Land Management. The legislature, usually quite stingy in the appropriation of state funds, voted $250,000 to pursue this cause in the courts. Nevada lawyers tried to build a case based on the dubious assumption that the state had been forced to renounce its claim to the public lands in 1864 as a condition of admission to the Union.

At first the rebellion energized local land barons and states' rights advocates. Several other states passed similar legislation, but without appropriations to fight the battle. Governor Ronald Reagan of California, then a candidate for president, announced that he too was a sagebrush rebel. But the movement soon lost momentum when many Nevadans became convinced that if such huge acreage were to become the property of the state government, it was more likely to be sold to real estate developers than to serve the livestock owners who had started the movement. Even Reagan, once he became president, was less than willing to dispose of the public lands in the manner that the rebels wanted. He apparently wanted to sell some of the land to the highest bidders to pay down the national debt. This idea had no traction with the sagebrush rebels. Their enterprise did not get a serious hearing in the federal courts, and soon fizzled.

Environmentalists won a modest defensive victory in this instance, deflecting a landgrab by one segment of land users. The federal government's stewardship agencies survived the diversionary episode. Most of Nevada remained under the federal government's stewardship agencies halfway through the first decade of the twenty-first century. The open question was whether the concept of federal protection of the resources could survive the relaxation of standards and change of priorities in Washington after 2001.

A few places exist where evidence of remedial conservation can be dramatic. In the Sheldon National Wildlife Refuge along the Nevada-Oregon border, overgrazing was the norm before the 1990s. Cattle were removed from this 571,000-acre tract in the mid-1990s, and the native species had a fighting chance to restore the terrain to the conditions that existed before the cattle empire arrived. Wet meadows and wildlife native to the area began to reappear. Likewise, in the Great Basin National Park in White Pine County, changes in grazing protocol made a substantial difference. Cattle grazing had been permitted for several years after the park was established in 1986, but later the government paid the ranchers to yield most of their grazing privileges. When most of the livestock were gone, the natural ecosystem of Lehman Creek seemed to be reviving.

The Friendly Polluters

One might consider the older mining towns nestled in remote canyons in the high country, such as Virginia City, Pioche, Austin, and Eureka, as examples of what the downsizing industrial revolution of the twentieth century did to the land and the people who made their homes there. The nineteenth-century mining frontier passed over this region like a storm cloud, leaving both refreshing moisture and damage behind. The industrial pollution was serious enough—mine dumps and mercury-polluted ponds below the mills remained from the 1870s—but most of the cedar, pine, and sagebrush landscape endured and recovered without extensive damage.

Yet any hiker on a roadway, in a canyon, or along a hillside in the vicinity of an old mining camp or farm settlement can find the junk of earlier visitors. The jettisoned trash is strewn in disgusting abundance in the most beautiful places that nature has provided in the high desert landscape. If one approaches a town on the highway, a grove of deciduous trees in a rocky canyon, or a mountain stream in a remote meadow—anyplace that invites a picnic or campsite—one will discover a pile of rubbish. Discarded beer cans and bottle fragments are usually most common. Rusted tin cans, bedsprings, remnants of plastic picnic gear, corroded fragments of auto chassis—all artifacts of a "use-it-and-toss-it" mentality—assault the eye.

We are learning to maintain our urban streets and parks in a systematic way in Las Vegas, Reno, and smaller Nevada cities and towns. Self-respecting suburbs and remote rural places are usually tidy at their inner cores. But many who use the public domain simply leave their waste behind. Garbage dumping continues to be a hazard. The final chapter of this book considers the efforts of federal and state agencies and various citizens' organizations to deal with such refuse.

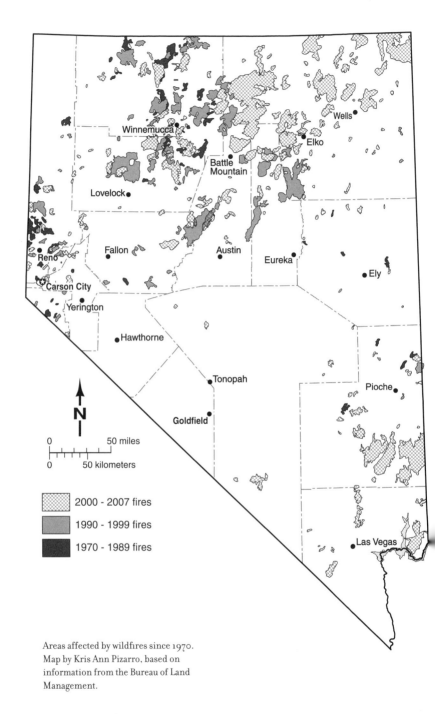

Areas affected by wildfires since 1970.
Map by Kris Ann Pizarro, based on
information from the Bureau of Land
Management.

FIRE! A Recurring Danger

For the rangelands and older mining camps, the most imminent and erratic threat to the familiar ecological terrain is from neither the military landgrabs nor the massive digs of contemporary excavators but rather the wildfires that rage with ever greater frequency in the valleys and mountains. If we study the history of any Nevada mining town in pioneer days, we find a record of fires that have scorched landscape, homes, and habitats. In fact, venerable mining camps often faced—and occasionally succumbed to—raging flames. The great fires in Pioche in 1871 and Goldfield in 1923 are examples of memorable mining-town blazes that raised the consciousness of residents. The Virginia City fire of 1875 that destroyed most of the early Comstock structures was the most infamous of the Nevada conflagrations. In that case, the district was still in bonanza, and investors were eager to pour money into rebuilding. Most other Nevada camps were not so fortunate.

Far more serious in recent decades have been the destructive brushland and forest fires. The arid valleys to the north—prime territory for livestock grazing—have been scorched by firestorms of increasing ferocity. In 1964 Elko County experienced a cluster of lightning strikes that burned more than 300,000 acres and brought firefighting crews from across the West. Humboldt County's ranges suffered a similar experience in the mid-1980s. The year 1999 was the most devastating year for destructive rural and rangeland fires in the state's history. The blazes that scorched Nevada's northern counties were without precedent. According to federal and state government agencies, more than 1.6 million acres of basin and range habitat burned over several weeks, mostly in northern Nevada. The Nevada Department of Wildlife reported that the total acreage burned was more than all the combined area that had been scorched in Nevada during the previous forty years. The effect on the flora and fauna was still being calculated several years later.

In the twenty-five years between 1980 and 2005, at least eighteen major fires occurred in the Carson Ranger district on the eastern slopes of the Sierra Nevada, north, east, and south of Lake Tahoe. A particularly dangerous forest-rangeland inferno occurred in 2004 on the edge of Carson City—virtually within the city-county limits. The political nerve center of the state extends beyond the familiar grid of government buildings and historic sites in Eagle Valley at the eastern base of the Sierra Nevada into western mountains. The inferno swept along the eastern foothills within two miles of the governor's mansion. Only a change in the winds and the diligence of the firefighters prevented an urban disaster.

In 2007 the Angora fire south of Lake Tahoe burned thousand of acres and destroyed more than two hundred homes in California—the most devastating blaze in the Sierra Nevada in many years. Two fires in the foothills west of Reno, fueled by dry terrain and high winds, also burned to the edge of the city. The U.S. Bureau of Land Management and the U.S. Forest Service have taken the lead in trying to protect communities and property against the ravages of blaze that can threaten both property and life (discussed further in chapter 8).

Some loggers and urban residents surmise that forests have become overgrown and thus are susceptible to such blazes. This hypothesis proposes that more underbrush should be cleared away. Environmentalists argue that the forests need to be thinned according to scientific guidelines, not for profit by those who would peel the living skin away.

Mountain and rangeland fires are more common and most devastating in periods of prolonged drought, such as those that occurred in the years between 2000 and 2007. Perhaps global warming—bringing hotter summers and warmer and drier winters—accounts for the drying up of our forests and rangelands and the scorching blazes we have experienced in recent years. The spread of urban and rural communities and increased use of the land for industrial and recreational purposes are also obvious factors in the increasing numbers of destructive fires.

CHAPTER TWO

The Mining Giveaway

In Nevada history precious-metal mining is in a privileged category. The silver bonanza that began in the early 1860s was one
justification for Nevada's hasty admission into the federal Union
in 1864. For the first half century of statehood, extracting and
processing silver and gold ore from underground shafts were the
state's primary enterprises. After an interval of a few decades, the
mining companies found a new cornucopia in open pits, with profound consequences for the natural landscape.

The First Bonanza: The Comstock Lode

When prospectors first panned for gold on the tiny tributaries
of the Carson River in the 1850s, they had little impact on the
land and water, only slightly greater than those who cultivated
the land farther upstream in Carson Valley near the verdant
Sierra Nevada. Washing and sifting the gold-bearing sand by
hand were slow, coaxing processes. In Nevada, placer mining
literally scratched the surface along the rivulets of the western
Great Basin.

These early gold hunters took the wealth from the earth by
gentle, careful washing of the sand. They were among the rugged

individualists of the West. We older Nevadans once admired them as much as we did the cowboys and sheepherders. Using only a pick, shovel, mortar, and pestle to extract the granules of ore that had tumbled down the slopes, the early miners broke, washed, and cradled their treasures a pan full at a time. Little wonder that a statue to the industrious miner stands in the capitol plaza in Carson City, a pick in his upraised arms, ready to force wealth from the earth by his manual labor.

Big changes occurred quickly, as was often the case on the western frontier. Underground mining methods matured in the Great Basin during the 1860s, at about the time the Central Pacific approached Nevada from the West, pointed toward a connection with the Union Pacific near the Great Salt Lake. The eastern slopes of the Sierra Nevada had not offered the same golden chances for quick profits that the canyons of California's mother lode region had provided to the mortar-and-pestle diggers. But with new technology, those who came first, or were most crafty, flourished.

Dynamite gouged the terrain, replacing the placer miner. Opening the Comstock Lode on Mount Davidson in 1860 brought new technology and promises of profitability, at a cost to the landscape. Tearing metals from underground, rather than coaxing them from the streams, became the norm. This process required digging shafts, hoisting the ore in large buckets, timbering the shafts with sturdy poles cut from the Sierra Nevada forests to make the deep caverns "safe," and feeding loads of cordwood into the steam-driven hoists. Hundreds of tons of ore were hauled down through the canyons to stamp mills on the Carson River, first by horse-drawn wagons and later by train. All of it took a toll on the forest resources of the mountain slopes.

Journalist Dan DeQuille, the foremost chronicler of the Comstock's glory days, wrote expansively of the achievements of the mining industry in *The Big Bonanza:*

The Comstock lode may truthfully be said to be the tomb of the forests of the Sierras. Millions on millions of feet of lumber are annually buried in the mines, never more to be resurrected. . . .

Not less than eighty million feet of timber and lumber are annually consumed on the Comstock lode. In a single mine—the Consolidated Virginia—timber is being buried at the rate of six million feet per annum, and in all other mines in like proportion. At the same time about 250,000 cords of wood are consumed. (174)

DeQuille also testified to the great quantities of mercury lost in the process of separating gold and silver from the crushed ore. Untold amounts flowed through the mills and into the Carson River despite dedicated efforts to retrieve it for reuse. He guessed that as much as 7,344,000 pounds had been lost in ten years of the bonanza era. More recent studies have assumed twice that amount had washed into the adjacent sands and fields. In our generation— 140 years later—scientists are calculating the cost to those living along the edges of the river and trying to clean up the toxins.

At the beginning of the twenty-first century, there was still no obvious solution to the environmental problem left by the nineteenth. The mercury is so widely scattered in the Carson River Basin that no workable method exists to retrieve it. Present and future generations are forced to live with the fact that the techniques used to extract the famed precious metals of the Comstock Lode left a legacy of poison in one of our precious rivers. As of 2009, this was Nevada's only "superfund cleanup site" designated by the federal government.

The resilient timberlands of the Sierra Nevada recovered, at least partially, from the logging of the nineteenth century. Even the poisonous material dumped into the Carson River may prove to be manageable if federal cleanup efforts are allowed to continue without budget cuts from administrations insensitive to past and future pollution.

The Legal Legacy: The Mining Law of 1872

Another delayed trauma was political and legal as well as environmental. Its ravaging effects were potentially as deadly as the immediate extraction policies. This was the federal mining law of 1872, a
primitive piece of legislation that continued to sanction rape of the
land 135 years after it was enacted.

The man most responsible for this legislation was Nevada's first
U.S. senator, William M. Stewart. He had studied law at Yale and
practiced in the courts of California's gold country before arriving
in the Great Basin in 1860 just as Nevada Territory was conceived.
His crafty politics, towering physical frame, sketchy legal training,
and on-the-ground knowledge of the mining frontier combined to
gain him a seat in the U.S. Senate immediately after Nevada's admission to the Union in 1864. He represented Nevada in the U.S.
Senate from 1864 to 1875 and again from 1887 to 1905.

Senator Stewart wrote much of the first national mining law,
enacted in 1866. It not only gave miners consent to trespass on
the public domain but also recognized that local rules (where they
were available) had the force of law. As modified later by the act of
1872, it froze in place the predatory instincts of the mining industry toward the land and water.

Every major effort to modify this law in later years was blocked
by senators from the western states, who were usually beholden to
the mining companies. For decades, Stewart, his associates, and his
successors defended the private exploiters of the rich minerals of
the West against the public interest. For a century after he retired
from Congress in 1905, senators from the Far West managed to
keep the core of this legislation on the law books, because those who
claimed mineral rights had clout with their senators in Washington.

Nevada's environment had a breather for twenty years after the
Comstock faded. The mining industry was almost dormant from
1880 until 1900. The low price of silver and the lack of investor
capital spared the state the kind of exploitation that had attended

its years of infancy. At the turn of the century, this period of exploitative lethargy ended.

The Second Bonanza: Tonopah and Goldfield

The discovery of silver at Tonopah in 1900 and gold in Goldfield in 1902 roused Nevada from its sleep. The two towns, only twenty-five miles apart, followed the standard for precious-metal mining that had existed earlier. Ores from Tonopah and Goldfield were extracted and processed in the old-fashioned way by "hard-rock" miners, usually hoisted from the shafts in buckets, then milled and processed nearby. The finished bullion went to its distant markets by railroad. The "second bonanza" was even more short-lived than the first. The boom had ended within a dozen years. By standards of the late twentieth century, the miners of Tonopah and Goldfield extracted and processed modest amounts of earth.

In retrospect, the environmental damage in those two districts was relatively small. One still sees the barren dumps and slag heaps, the inorganic waste of Tonopah that does not decompose. They are even regarded as colorful by some history buffs. No long-range, long-distance toxic legacy has yet been identified from these operations. A similar summary could be made for other modest-size mining operations in the early years of the twentieth century in Pioche, Searchlight, Delamar, and Rhyolite. That statement would not be appropriate for the next stage of Great Basin mining history.

New Technology: Big Pits and Long Hauls
White Pine Copper

Before 1900 prospectors discovered outcroppings of copper ore in the Egan Range west of Ely. They attracted little interest before 1900 because the rock was "low grade." This was tantalizing to investors, who now sought something other than precious metals. In 1900, when copper prices were attractive because the value of the ore was rising, the original claims passed into the hands of large out-of-state investors who extracted the ore in giant shovels and huge trucks.

The most promising site for a mill and smelter was twenty miles east, at the ranch of William McGill, a man who had engaged in raising livestock. Mining developers purchased this green oasis and constructed a railroad between their pit and smelter, renaming the new town site McGill. Planning for the mill and smelter began about 1905; the results were more advanced than anything previously seen in Nevada. The developers began producing the refined metal in 1908. Within a dozen years, the ore from White Pine was yielding refined copper of greater value than the gold and silver being produced in Tonopah and Goldfield. The minerals were valued in hundreds of millions of dollars in the first half century of operation, as copper was in great demand as the nation increased its production and use of electricity, for which copper was an excellent conductor. Like other open-pit mines, the McGill mine operated for about seventy-five years, enjoying times of prosperity (especially during the two world wars) and enduring periods of loss (especially during the Great Depression and in the 1950s).

At the site of the ore deposits, engineers decided the most efficient way to extract the minerals was by the open-pit method rather than shafts that pursued rich veins, which had been the standard method in the late nineteenth century in Nevada. The open-pit method ripped massive gouges in the mountain with gigantic mechanized shovels, then trucked the overburden to the surface to spread it across adjacent hillsides. The scars of seven decades of open-pit mining are prominent features along U.S. Highway 50 for several miles west of Ely. The deeper the pits became, the more costly the operation and the greater the overburden to be hauled away and dumped in nearby canyons and hillsides. The original town of Ruth, established in 1904, had to be relocated several times to accommodate the digging.

Near the mill and smelter twenty miles east of the gaping pits at Ruth, environmental damage was more serious. Tailings from the mill washed down into the Steptoe Valley to the west. Sludge from the smelter accumulated on the slopes not far from the company town where the workers and managers lived. Russell Elliott, a native of McGill and Nevada's foremost historian of mining, recalled his childhood days when dust from the tailings pit whirled into the town as prevailing westerly winds blew across the "white sands" area: "This huge area of milling and smelting wastes had developed as an easy way of disposing of such materials by letting gravity take residues from the bench area to the valley floor, a drop of 50 to 100 feet. Little, if any, thought was given to any possible effects of the decision on the town and its inhabitants. The main consideration was to get the ore reduced to metal as quickly and effectively as possible in order to insure the best returns on the investment" (*Growing Up* 46–47). In springtime and summer, when the westerly winds were prevalent, this dust was the curse of housewives, who could not keep the insides of their houses free of the drifting dirt. "It seeped through the doors and window onto the floors, woodwork, furniture, dishes and cooking utensils, and clothing, and into eyes, noses, mouths, lungs, ears and hair" (47).

In addition to the "white sands" from the mill, there were the "black sands" from the smelter, less attractive but also less volatile on windy days. At times the company tried to cover the white sands with black sands, with little beneficial effect. Eventually, the company tried to plant vegetation on the sands after adding nutrients. This reduced the problem temporarily as long as water was provided.

In the early 1970s, the McGill smelter was found to be in violation of federal clean-air standards. Atmospheric emissions from the smelter failed to meet the standards set by the federal Clean Air Act of 1970. After a struggle in the government agencies and with the price of copper depressed in the world markets, the copper producers ended their mining in 1978 and closed their smelters in 1983.

Yerington Copper

The next large copper producer in Nevada was smaller with a shorter lifespan than the White Pine enterprise, but the toxic results became evident more quickly. Another ecological bad dream emerged at the old Anaconda mine in the Singatse Mountains near Yerington. This district yielded some ore during World War I and showed greater promise to developers in the years of World War II, when copper ore was in high demand and deep underground drilling had become standard practice in the search for needed minerals.

Anaconda Copper Mining Company, an international corporate giant, came on the scene in the late 1940s. Preparing for full production in the early years of the Korean War when the red metal was again in short supply, the company established a new town named Weed Heights, offering hundreds of jobs. New homes went up, boosting the economy of Lyon County to unprecedented levels of prosperity in the 1960s and 1970s. Huge earthmoving equipment created another huge pit at Weed Heights, immediately west of fertile Mason Valley and the small city of Yerington. Eventually, the site of the pit and processing plant enveloped thirty-five hundred acres.

Anaconda operated successfully for more than twenty years before it began to succumb to increasing costs of production and falling prices for copper. Ore was trucked to the railroad and shipped to Montana for smelting. Title to the property eventually shifted to ARCO and still later to another company that went bankrupt. After the mine and mill closed in the 1980s, the Weed Heights industrial plant stood dormant for several years. Home owners and renters continued to live in the community that Anaconda had built near the mine.

But a time bomb was ticking. To enrich the copper ore, substantial quantities of uranium had been used. The processing concentrated the uranium as it isolated the copper. By the early 2000s analysts recognized that the site had been contaminated by substantial amounts of radioactive material and other toxins resulting from the waste uranium.

Two decades after the mining and milling had ended, the struggle to ascertain who was responsible for mitigation of the contaminants accelerated. The search for responsible parties to pay for the cleanup brought the usual pattern of accusations and finger-pointing. The Bureau of Land Management took the lead in searching for a solution, as it had management and oversight responsibilities for some of the affected land. The Nevada Department of Environmental Protection (NDEP) also played a role, since some of the land was privately owned. The federal Environmental Protection Agency (EPA) also became involved in seeking a remedy.

In the meantime, local citizens were alarmed by the dust that regularly blew from Weed Heights on the windward side of Mason Valley. Just as troubling were reports that well water serving the community contained concentrations of uranium higher than those recommended by federal standards. Security guards were placed at the site to discourage the curious from approaching the most heavily contaminated areas. Nonetheless, the Yerington story turned out to be relatively small (at least in 2008) compared to one that emerged a few miles south of Las Vegas.

Basic, Henderson, and Gabbs

Applying Nevada standards of success in the mineral-processing realm, Henderson is the most remarkable example of survival and urban resurrection in the history of the state. Most mining and milling towns blossomed briefly on the desert and then crumbled into dust with the end of the booms that spawned them. The typical early mining camps resembled the colorful flowers that flourish in the springtime and wilt quickly in the summer's heat.

Basic was born as a magnesium-processing site in 1941; its workers and facilities had fulfilled its purpose in less than three years. But it had an afterlife like no other community on the

Nevada mining and milling frontier. A half century after its founding, Henderson (known as Basic until about 1953) was the second largest city in the state, one of the fastest-growing urban centers in the nation, with a highly diversified industrial economy. On its official fiftieth birthday in 2003, Henderson was a metropolis spread across 100 square miles, with a population estimated at 225,000. It had not only survived the boom-and-bust pattern of the mining-milling industry but also turned that cliché on its head.

Henderson had a more exotic beginning than any of its sibling communities to the north. When the U.S. government evaluated wartime needs and resources before World War II, it became aware of a critical shortage of magnesium, a metal essential for lightweight airplane parts and explosives. A promising source of this ore existed at Paradise Mountain near Gabbs Valley, a remote desert highlands area 350 miles northwest of Las Vegas. The nearest convenient source of water and power for giving final refinement to the mineral was in Las Vegas Valley, near Boulder (later Hoover) Dam. In the extraction process, geologists probed Paradise Mountain at Gabbs with diamond drills, and earthmovers enlarged the pit. The ore was concentrated at a mill at the site before it was hauled to Basic, leaving the residue on the site.

The mastermind of the Gabbs-Basic enterprise was Howard Eells, president of Basic Refractories, Inc., a metallurgical firm based in Cleveland, Ohio. It held a patent for producing aluminum from refractory bricks. Using technology learned from Germany and the United Kingdom, the company re-created itself as Basic Magnesium, Inc. (BMI), in 1940 and, with U.S. government help, built a huge plant in the southern part of Las Vegas Valley.

The direct-route distance between Gabbs and Las Vegas in 1940 was a bumpy trek over mostly unpaved, hot, dusty roads. The federal highway building program initiated during the Great Depression had barely begun to affect the Great Basin. The option first chosen for moving the ore from Gabbs to the Basic Magnesium plant was overland by railroad. The magnesite and brucite ores were extracted from a huge pit at Gabbs, crushed, concentrated, and roasted. Originally, the product was trucked southward to Luning, where a spur of the Southern Pacific remained from the days of the Tonopah bonanza. From Luning, the cargo followed the railroad along an irregular 270-degree arc to Fernley, Winnemucca, Elko, Ogden, Salt Lake City, and eventually the Las Vegas Valley—a distance of 1,148 miles. Later, as the rough automobile roads were improved, concentrated ore was moved in massive trucks a much shorter distance by a more direct route, an almost straight line from Gabbs to the final refining plant at Basic. It went southeasterly across the most arid stretch of Nevada to a barren site a dozen miles south of Las Vegas, a distance of 343 miles.

The Basic Magnesium plant soon became the largest industrial facility and employer in Nevada's history. The massive gray industrial structures that rose ominously in the valley south of Las Vegas became a distasteful centerpiece to the community that clustered around it. Basic-Henderson was another Nevada boomtown, but this time the U.S. government was the grubstaker (the label used by prospectors for the benefactors who provided money for bacon and beans while they searched the mountains for ore). Uncle Sam had far more resources to spend during the war years than any grubstaker of former times. Within two years of completion, the Basic plant was producing more refined magnesium than necessary for defense purposes. As a wartime-production enterprise, it was abundantly successful.

The area's mundane social and political details are well documented in standard historical sources. Much of the personal drama and industrial details remain available in photographs. Missing from this panorama of historical data are discussions of the chemical consequences. The manufacture of magnesium was far more complicated than any metallurgical enterprise previously undertaken in Nevada. It involved more than roasting ore at Gabbs before transporting the concentrates to Henderson. At that point the concentrate met thousands of acre-feet of water that had been pumped and piped from Lake Mead through a massive government-funded conduit. For several months 30 million gallons a day flowed into the BMI plant. Massive quantities of salt came from Death Valley and other California dry lakes to accelerate the process. A 200,000-kilowatt transmission line was built from Boulder Dam into the Basic plant.

There the witches' brew became more complex. The concentrate from Gabbs was mixed with peat moss (mostly from British Columbia) and crushed coal (mostly from northern Utah), chlorinated in hot furnaces, and transformed into molten magnesium chloride as the chlorine was baked off. Uncounted tons of refuse flowed or sifted into the nearby desert. The refined magnesium ingots moved on to distant defense plants for further wartime production. No precious metal boomtown of Nevada had ever produced so abundantly for such a focused purpose.

After the war, the U.S. government had no further use for this massive industrial infrastructure, so Nevada's political leaders, led by Senator Pat McCarran, arranged a quick sale of the assets. The state government bought part of the site for a bargain price and re-sold it to private interests. Both Congress and the 1947 session of the Nevada legislature enacted the legal authority for this handoff, which cost the State of Nevada very little. Within a few years, a significant shift in ownership had been made. The company town of "Basic" evolved into the community of Henderson, chartered and anointed as an incorporated city under the laws of Nevada in 1953. Among the early buyers and operators were companies that processed titanium, alkali, and other chemicals. Some were clean and environmentally friendly. Some became another land mine waiting to detonate or a slow seepage polluter whose toxic legacy would be known only decades later.

Nevada's historians paid little attention to the environmental consequences of the Basic-Henderson bonanza and its sequel. One notable exception is William T. Dobbs, a New Yorker transplanted to Nevada in the 1980s. He published a prophetic analysis of the situation in 1991 that has gained little notice, "Southern Nevada and the Legacy of Basic Magnesium, Incorporated." The Dobbs article offers a panoramic view—industrial and social—of the community's evolution. It still deserves mention nearly two decades later because it touches on the environmental issues that other historians have overlooked.

As concentrates were processed at Basic Magnesium in the 1940s, the chlorination plant often experienced leaks when pipe seals proved inadequate. Crucibles used to bake the ores often cracked. Such events regularly produced hazards for the workers, who also endured excessive heat. Part of the problem was handled by blowing the chlorine vapors—a greenish yellow gas—upward into the atmosphere. Men and women who worked in the plant wore masks and tried peppermint and tobacco chews to reduce the discomfort. Downwind residents often smelled the pollutants in the air. They were assured that no permanent health damage would occur. Most were unaware that chlorine gas was one of the agents present in the poison gas attacks of World War I that killed thousands of soldiers on the fields of France. The Basic plant continued to produce chlorine even after its magnesium operations had been closed, because there were other commercial uses for the gas. Some of its units were soon converted to yield products such as aluminum chloride, molybdenum, and hydrochloric acid. One of more profitable and potentially dangerous yields of the Henderson facility was perchlorate. (We will resume our discussion of this toxin in chapter 4.)

Local governments and chambers of commerce struggled for decades to put the best face on the prospects of Henderson, and they had much to commend their efforts. The southern part of the Las Vegas Valley offers a panorama of great beauty and many resources left behind by the government. Henderson expanded and prospered from the luxuriant developments at Green Valley.

Then, on May 8, 1988, a small fire at the factory of Pacific Engineering and Production Company (PEPCON) ignited a blast that

destroyed the factory and caused massive damage to nearby property. It seemed miraculous that the event killed only two people and
injured only three hundred, because it registered as a medium-
scale earthquake in distant California seismic laboratories. Nearby schools and homes were evacuated; much residential property
was damaged. It was as if a devastating bomb had been dropped,
which, in a political sense, it had. The PEPCON incident was a wake-
up call for Nevadans—at least those living in southern Nevada. For
several years the region was on red alert. PEPCON relocated to a different site in a remote area of southern Utah, and worries about
the environmental dangers receded. In 1991 another incident at
the industrial plant involved the release of chlorine gas and the
evacuation of homes and schools.

In the last quarter century of the twentieth century, smaller and
(presumably) more environmentally friendly operations came
to Henderson. Newer tenants included medical services and industries, a pharmacy college, software firms, bakeries, and candy
makers. The Henderson Redevelopment Agency made a noble
and partially successful effort to overcome the blight and decay of
the early years. Residents of the city tried to erase the old Basic
smokestack image by introducing palm trees (although palm trees
are not indigenous to the area and are usually imported from
Mexico). Between 1980 and 2000 the periphery of Henderson
became more luxuriant than most of the rest of Las Vegas Valley.
Newer neighborhoods look more like southern California, trying
to overpower the lingering impressions of the area's primitive industrial period. The citizens of Henderson worked hard to change
the image of their community from a rusting industrial town to an
inviting "place to call home," as they described it in an attractive
document published in 2004 to commemorate the golden anni-
versary of the incorporation of the city. For several years in the
1990s, Henderson claimed to be one of the fastest-growing cities
in the nation.

The Third Bonanza: "Invisible" Gold

Forty years ago most Nevadans thought of the gold and silver bo-
nanzas as romantic memories from the distant past. The once
famous mining towns of Virginia City, Gold Hill, Tonopah, Goldfield, and Pioche were dormant. Even the vast copper mines and
smelters of White Pine County had suspended work, hoping for a
day when improved metal prices would allow them to resume. During the last quarter of the twentieth century, however, the mining
business came full circle—back to the quest that brought the '49ers
across the Great Basin in the first place. Raw gold, so fine it could
not be recognized by the older assaying methods, proved to be
available in abundance in the Great Basin. The earth-processing
industry made another quantum leap in the 1980s, extracting
minuscule amounts of the ore from mountains that were literally
moved and stripped of their precious contents.

Whereas Nevada's early silver mines and later copper and lead-
zinc mines had yielded small amounts of gold, the "yellow" metal
was seldom sought for its own sake within the borders of the state.
(The spectacular but short-lived boom at Goldfield after 1900 was
an exception.) In the late 1970s, however, with the price of gold
soaring on the world market and more aggressive metallurgy and
earthmoving techniques available, northern Nevada became the
center of a highly sophisticated gold rush. In terms of the earth
displaced and gold produced, it put all the previous mining booms
of the Far West in the shadows. In the short run, rural Nevada has
profited from this transition. Let's consider first the benefits and
later the concerns.

The Upside

The raw statistics are impressive. Nevada's mines have been first
in the United States and second or third in the world in the value of
gold produced for several years. In 2003 the state's mines yielded

82 percent of the gold produced in the United States and 9 percent of the world's total. During the same period the Silver State was in second place among U.S. states in the value of nonfuel minerals produced, outdone only by California. The total value of the refined ore was more than $3.2 billion. Nevada also led all other states in the production of silver in the 1990s.

The minuscule, widely dispersed specks of precious metals were and are extracted from more than a hundred mines—some of them gaping pits that on a clear day can be seen from airliners at thirty thousand feet. Gargantuan shovels and trucks raise the earth from far below the levels of the deepest shafts that the old hard-rock miners of Nevada ever probed.

Mining companies emphasize the benefits of this scenario. Nearly nine thousand men and women are employed directly by the mining and earth-processing units; thousands more provide services to the industry and payrolls to the communities they serve. Without this activity a vast swath of central Nevada would be impoverished by the decline of the more traditional livestock and mining activities.

The most prominent mining companies and the Nevada Mining Association (NMA) have repeatedly offered assurances that their use and restoration of the land are ecologically sound as well as economically beneficial. The industry claims that contemporary exploration technologies, plus advanced chemical and biological processes, make it possible to extract precious metals with minimal damage to the land. It claims expenditures of millions of dollars restoring the ecosystem and protecting sites for native flora and fauna. In many cases where huge displacements of earth have obliterated existing mountains, new mounds have risen to replace them. The producers of refined metals affirm that their restoration work often exceeds legal requirements; their critics claim that the standards in Nevada are too low. The mining industry often repeats the mantra that the amount of land directly affected by mining in Nevada is only one-tenth of 1 percent of the state's total area.

The Downside

At least three types of hazards exist in Nevada for the immediate and long-term future because of the mines: physical scars and dislocations of the earth caused by the sheer volume of rock and overburden being moved, the dewatering of the deep mines and accumulation of toxic waters in pits and underground, and mercury pollution in the earth and the atmosphere caused by the discharges from the smelters.

Physical Dislocations. Dramatic evidence of the short-term dangers appeared in February 1995, when a huge rock slide occurred at Newmont's Gold Quarry mine, north of Carlin, blocking a state highway for more than a quarter mile. Whether this was an exceptional event or a portent is a matter of debate.

Disturbance and Pollution of Water Tables. During the 1870s, the so-called palmy days of the "deep mines" of Virginia City and Pioche, the presence of underground water was a serious obstacle to profitable extraction of the ores. Too often pumps stoked by local trees broke down or wore out. In those cases mining companies usually abandoned their quests. The available technology was not equal to the commercial challenge of mining and selling the ore. In the twentieth and twenty-first centuries, the deep pits presented a comparable challenge, but huge pumps fueled by petroleum imported from half a world away lifted the underground aquifers with ease and sent their discharge down the Humboldt River or stored it in pits.

The preferred method of refining ore for the past quarter century has been "heap-leaching." This involves crushing the raw ore, piling it on a pad, and spraying it with a solution containing cyanide, which then percolates down through the heap for several weeks, leaching out the gold. The gold-enriched solution is then drained into a pond, from which it is pumped or otherwise transferred to smelting units. Inevitably in the process, cyanide-polluted water escapes into the ground or into containment ponds.

Because of the volume of earth moved and treated, the amounts of cyanide and acid left behind are huge. The "heap-leaching" process has become the favorite method of extracting gold because it is relatively inexpensive and requires a minimum of human labor. The cost of turning the microscopic particles of raw ore into refined metal that glistens on the world market is low. The cost to the earth is incalculable at this point.

Atmospheric Mercury Pollution. Another hazardous pollutant is the mercury released into the atmosphere from the gold-refining operations. The federal Environmental Protection Agency determined in the late 1990s that the smokestacks of four leading producers of gold in northern Nevada were belching forth dangerous amounts of this deadly toxin. The EPA has estimated that between 1998 and 2001 Nevada mining operations released more than twenty-one thousand pounds of mercury into the air annually, making Nevada the nation's leading source of atmospheric mercury pollution. Reports of this kind caused alarm in Utah and Idaho, which are often affected by winds passing over the Great Basin. The Idaho Conservation League has reported an alarming increase in the amount of mercury found in fish taken from that state's streams and lakes in recent years. Utah environmental authorities also detected serious increases in mercury in the Great Salt Lake and in the birds that feed on the lake's brine shrimp.

Four leading Nevada gold-producing companies agreed in 2001 to a voluntary reduction in the amount of mercury toxins released from their plants. "Scrubbers" were installed in their equipment in order to intercept the dangerous agents. Spokesmen for the Nevada Mining Association said there had been a substantial decrease in the toxin being released, but conservationists questioned whether adequate measurements were being made about the amounts of mercury being used, lost, and recovered in the smelting process. The fact remained that Nevada, because of its gold-mining industry, was by far the largest source of toxic mercury emissions into the atmosphere as the twenty-first century began.

Whatever remedial procedures were in place had not registered on the environmental charts halfway through the first decade of the new century.

Opportunity: The Fraser Institute, 2008

Nevada continued to offer unusual opportunities for the mining industry. The Fraser Institute of Canada, a private organization that conducts annual surveys of business opportunities around the world, for more than a decade has consistently ranked Nevada among the top five most favorable jurisdictions in the world for mining investment. In making its rankings, the Fraser Institute considers environmental regulations, taxation, infrastructure, political stability, native land claims, labor issues, and geological attractiveness (Sudol, "The Republic of Mining"). This means that Nevada's laws and attitudes toward mineral developers are lenient and the prospects for finding ore are good. In many places, regulatory duplication or awkward local conditions create a hostile climate for development.

Elko County and other parts of northern Nevada have been ideal venues for the mining companies since the 1970s. The mineral potential was high, the area was remote from heavily populated areas, state and local governmental regulations were simple and affable, and the prevailing political attitudes favored the investors. The northern tier of counties had become the most conservative part of the state, the birthplace of the "Sagebrush Rebellion" and a seedbed of radical defiance of federal policies to protect the environment. It was fertile ground for the developers, that is, mineral exploiters and prospectors. The largest gold mining companies have reported to their investors and potential clients that the ground they are mining has reserves that will sustain their production profitably for the next fifteen or twenty years. This means the procedures they are using to extract and refine the ore can be expected to continue for another quarter century, at least. Since the 1950s oil-producing companies have also searched for the "black gold" beneath the valleys of eastern Nevada, but to date (perhaps fortunately) they have found very little.

The demographic facts of life in Nevada put a different face on the situation. Clark County and the Reno, Sparks, and Carson City regions, where more than 80 percent of the people of the state live, are hundreds of miles distant from the regions where the largest mining companies are extracting and processing gold. The state's most dangerous industrial and military experiments have typically been conducted beyond the horizon. Thus, it is easy for "the public" to give their attention to those matters that seem more urgent at the moment.

Dr. Vernon Scheid, longtime dean of the Mackay School of Mines in Reno who offered many speeches and professional papers, was fond of saying, "If you can't grow it, you have to mine it." His message is, of course, that modern civilization requires the use of the world's resources for our modern comfort and amenities. This motto is often repeated by the minerals-production fraternity. University of Nevada–Reno scholars Peter Goin and C. Elizabeth Raymond enhanced this slogan by enumerating the countless modern devices dependent on earth minerals for their production: toasters, telephones, television sets, bridges, high-rise buildings, razor blades, modern roads, and medicine, ad infinitum (xvii). The authors were focusing our attention on the nonprecious minerals, not the gold and silver that have justified much of Nevada's production. But the essential point is the same. Can we find better ways to extract and process metals and minerals needed by contemporary civilization? That is the question that contemporary environmentalists are asking.

CHAPTER THREE

The Northern Waters

Nevadans have an uneasy relationship with the waters that make their desert cultures possible. We take our lakes, rivers, and underground sources for granted—like an unnoticed bloodstream that seems to be functioning well. Only when these channels fail to flow adequately do most of us give them serious attention. The host bodies—whether individual humans, farms, or cities—often abuse their arteries. Desert dwellers often insist on the amenities of the green, luxuriant eastern venues, without regard for the long-term consequences. They remember their health only when it is threatened.

In this arid state, with rainfall of only about three inches per year in Las Vegas and seven in the more favored valleys of the Northwest, most of us are water wasters, but reluctant to face that fact. In the recent past, public planning for the careful use of this scarce resource has improved the pattern, but it is only partially successful. In the late 1990s the state government had a Division of Water Planning within the Department of Conservation and Natural Resources. It produced an excellent, comprehensive plan for careful monitoring of water usage (*Nevada State Water Plan*, March 1999). Shortly thereafter the state government abolished the office, transferring its duties to the Nevada Department of Environmental Protection. This termination had the support of leaders of both parties in the legislature. Protests of environmentalists had no effect. Much speculation has flowed from this decision. Was the office abolished because its findings were too controversial, or did the political leaders decide its work could be better done in a larger agency? This judgment must be left to diligent student-researchers.

The habit of carefully saving and then wasting the West's most precious resource evolved not only from the practices of the earliest settlers but also from Native Americans, miners, town builders, and livestock men. Let us consider what modern practices have done to four waterways of northern Nevada: the Carson, Truckee, Walker, and Humboldt. We will return to the Colorado River in a subsequent chapter.

Carson River: Bonanza Pollution and Political "Reclamation"

The Carson River flows northeast from two main sources several miles apart in the forests of the central Sierra Nevada of eastern California; the east and west forks converge in the region where Nevada was born. Near the point where the two streams meet in Carson Valley, Mormon Station (later renamed Genoa) was established in 1851. From there the natural course of the river continues northeasterly, until it ends in the alkaline Carson Sink, a region that resembles the Dead Sea. The total length is about 180 miles.

For seven or eight years in the 1850s, the Mormons shared the river and the region with itinerant emigrants and prospectors; the latter were placer miners from the goldfields of California, who panned for gold on a tributary downstream near another settlement, first called Chinatown and later Dayton. The Carson River was the route preferred by most who trekked overland from the eastern states, seeking the goldfields of California.

This scenario was chaotic—especially in late summer when flowing water was scarce. But the Carson River's rustic charm provided raw material for the romantic melodrama of later generations. Gold-bearing sand, like that in the Mother Lode country of California, could be coaxed from the gullies near the Carson River. Since the number of prospectors was small in the 1850s, environmental disturbance was slight.

In the 1860s new rumors spread across the mountains: there was a "monster ledge" rich in gold and silver ore in the high country just east of the Sierra Nevada. The rock could be torn from the earth by new methods, hauled down the canyon in large wagons, and crushed and milled on the river. All these techniques were innovations that transformed the West; they had enormous consequences for the future.

Local historians once took pride in documenting the fact that Nevadans helped invent the new methods of extracting, hauling, and processing precious ore. A few noted that the benefits flowed—while they were still flowing—away from the land of origin. Fewer still recognized that ecological damage caused by the mines and milling remained behind. Modern technology had reached the bucolic banks of the Carson River with only the faintest concern for its refuse.

As the mine owners sank shafts and dug tunnels in search of the hidden wealth of the Comstock Lode, they spared no cost—human, monetary, or environmental—in their quest for lucre. While producing the half-billion dollars of precious metal prior to 1880, the mining men not only ravaged the forests of the Sierra Nevada and the sparse flora of the local mountains but also did lasting damage to the Carson River. They left behind, like the dumps from the mines and garbage of the mills and smelter, a legacy of exploited streams and sick, burned-out miners.

Dan DeQuille, whose testimony about the devastation of the Sierra Nevada forests I noted earlier, may serve as our witness once again. Reflecting on the loss of quicksilver (mercury) in the milling process, he found a mystery. Large quantities of the liquid metal were brought into the mills to force the separation of the precious metals from the "country rock" as it was being washed and steamed for refinement. Although most of the gold and silver was presumably retrieved, only a fraction of the mercury was successfully caught to be reused, even though diligent efforts were made to recycle it. As DeQuille wrote in *The Big Bonanza:* "It is an axiom among millmen that 'wherever quicksilver is lost, silver is lost'; therefore there must be a large amount of silver lost. . . . The amount of quicksilver used by the mills working the Comstock ores alone averages 800 flasks of $76\frac{1}{2}$ pounds each; or 61,000 pounds per month. This in one year would amount to 734,400 pounds of quicksilver that go somewhere, and counting backwards for ten years shows 7,344,000 pounds that have *gone* somewhere—either up the flue or down the flume" (98). It has been estimated that Comstock millers lost a pound of mercury for each ton of ore they processed. Recent analysis of the Carson River riverbed shows that much poisonous residue settled in the stream, later to be found in alarming quantities in the fish.

Entrepreneurs such as William Sharon and Adolph Sutro personified the industrial revolution in western Nevada in the 1860s. Ambitious, power hungry, eager to manipulate men and women as well as the environment, they brought money, skills, and a desire to do what was necessary for profit. They and other moneyed barons worked their will for twenty years, leaving thousands of tons of tailings in the river bottom as well as the debris from their shafts on Mount Davidson. A century after the promoters were gone and the riches had left Nevada, the pollutants remained. The residue of mercury in the Carson River caused it to be the only federal "superfund" site in Nevada (as mentioned in chapter 2).

The Newlands Era

The next substantial change for the Carson River occurred after 1902, when Nevada congressman Francis G. Newlands, Sharon's son-in-law and heir, managed to get a landmark reclamation act approved in Congress. Having tried for a decade to sell his idea of a nationally funded irrigation program for the arid West, he finally won his uphill battle. When Theodore Roosevelt became president in 1901, Newlands had a powerful ally for his cause in the White House.

The Newlands Project required damming the Carson River downstream and joining its waters with those of the Truckee (its northern neighbor) and then diverting much of their waters farther eastward into the desert. Such a merger of these streams had not occurred for centuries, since the Pleistocene Lake Lahontan had covered the region. Our narrative about the Carson must pause here to introduce the upstream fate of its sibling, the Truckee.

The Truckee Basin: Two Lakes and Two Destinations

The 140-mile Truckee River is the most notorious watershed in the Great Basin, if we examine the historical and legal blotters. It was the last segment of the trail that led the Donner party of 1846 to its deadly fate in the Sierra Nevada, earning a bad reputation almost from the time of its discovery. It generated the greatest controversy and sustained the greatest environmental change among the small river systems of northern Nevada in the twentieth century. It is the aorta of Reno. Pouring its waters through the center of the Biggest Little City in the World, it shared the unsavory reputation of that once scandalous municipality. But it had an innocent beginning.

Lake Tahoe

Lake Tahoe, the main source of the Truckee River, is an azure jewel set like a precious stone within the verdant forests of the high Sierra Nevada. Poets and artists have often tried to capture its dazzling beauty in word or paint. The surrounding forested basin embraces about 500 square miles, the lake itself about 190—which is a large body of freshwater by the standards of the desert West. The California-Nevada boundary slices though the lake, divided about 65 percent for California and 35 percent for Nevada.

During the bonanza years in Virginia City and Gold Hill, the timberlands around Lake Tahoe and in the Carson Range were aggressively harvested. A complex network of loggers, sawmills, flumes, and railroad links moved the tall trees into the depths of the mines. Dan DeQuille called the underground workings of the Comstock a "tomb" for the forests.

Mark Twain was one of the first pioneers to enjoy and exploit Tahoe. He staked a timber claim as he admired the pristine beauty of the lake in 1861. He extolled the purity of the air, which, in his joke, was similar to that breathed by the angels. When his campfire ignited a roaring forest blaze, he found it amusing. So it has been in this delicate basin—a struggle to exploit, enjoy, and preserve its natural richness, all at the same time.

For the past hundred years, Tahoe has been a jousting arena in the ongoing struggle between those who want to build homes, roads, businesses, and casinos and those who would try to preserve its natural beauty. The battle has been persistent, but uneven, and nature has been the loser.

Until the 1940s the lake and its surrounding basin remained mostly unspoiled. At midcentury, the pattern changed. When World War II ended and gasoline rationing was lifted, Americans hit the road again, seeking new vistas. "Better" roads were cut along the rugged Tahoe shoreline, and national publicity brought tens of thousands of tourists and investors. Tahoe was under siege by the 1960s. A long period of development, lamentation, and quarreling finally led to the creation of the Tahoe Regional Planning Agency (TRPA) in 1970, established by Congress with the approval of the legislatures of California and Nevada. Those who fashioned the compromise that became TRPA had to deal with the arguments of the gambling tycoons and other developers who were crowding into the north and south ends of the lake. Casinos and motels had become larger, up-scale businesses and homes more luxurious. Refuse and silt inevitably flowed into the lake.

The epic struggle over the future of Lake Tahoe has been well documented by Douglas H. Strong, historian laureate of the Tahoe Basin. One might cautiously conclude that TRPA has been partially successful in retarding "development" and making it more responsible, but the ecological health of the basin and lake has continued to decline.

Tahoe is one of the largest high-mountain, deep-blue forested lakes on the planet. It is also a laboratory for experimenting, on a local scale, on ecological problems common around the world. In the meantime, the permanent year-round population of the lake region has risen to sixty-five thousand, mostly in upscale homes. Hundreds of thousands of tourists visit the basin every year, enjoying its beauty and creating air-pollution problems and causing ongoing damage to the forests.

The Truckee River

After it leaves Lake Tahoe, the Truckee tumbles down its narrow, rugged canyon for about thirty miles before it slows down and relaxes near the Nevada-California state line. On the Nevada side, the more level basin terrain gives the river a rest from its frenetic surge along the rocky channel from the Tahoe outlet. After meandering through the Truckee Meadows (Reno and Sparks) in a leisurely manner, the river ambles or sometimes trickles toward its original destination—the mysterious Pyramid Lake. Then it is interrupted a few miles downstream and diverted for its shotgun wedding to the Carson River. In this merger, another century-old controversy arose.

Because its main sources are on the California side of Lake Tahoe and its original destination was Pyramid Lake, the Truckee River shares the complex history of those two scenic siblings. They are as dissimilar as any two linked bodies of water in North America. From the alpine splendor of the Tahoe Basin to the desert setting of Pyramid (which resembles the Dead Sea of Palestine and has been used by Hollywood filmmakers to represent Old Testament settings), it runs the gauntlet from mountain majesty to biblical desert. Leaving the lake at its northern edge, it passes the remains of logging operations, sawmills, rusting electric-generating plants, headgates for irrigation ditches, and Reno and Sparks diversions and pollutions. Fortunately, most of these ventures came and went before they did lasting damage to the channel.

When it reaches its natural destination, the Truckee's sluggish flow serves the impoverished Paiute Indian Reservation. Here a few hundred tenacious Native Americans have tried to rescue enough ditch water to build a traditional economy based on the early values of the tribe—to retain their fishery and to cultivate the land—which are conflicting purposes on this terrain. The Paiutes have recently built an informative museum to honor their culture.

To seek a better understanding of the Truckee River's history, we must work our way back upstream as the cutthroat trout once did, seeking the northwest quadrant of Lake Tahoe. Here the main channel of the river debouches over the rim on its journey northward. At this point the first major alteration of the natural life of the river occurred in 1870–1871.

In the 1860s San Francisco promoter Allexey Von Schmidt established the Lake Tahoe and San Francisco Water Works Company. It was a bold plan to divert the river *westward* through a series of canals, flumes, and pipes from the high mountains to the city on the bay. Von Schmidt promoted this scheme for more than 30 years, until 1900, without success. Early in this enterprise he built a dam at the outlet of the lake, raising its level six feet above the natural rim, with a mechanism for holding or releasing the water as the managers of the dam dictated.

As snowmelt from the high Sierra Nevada peaks flowed in behind this barricade, the dam changed the nature of the lake, creating a reservoir in those top six feet. This became the main resource for the valleys of western Nevada. For most of the past 140 years, the shoreline of the lake has been higher than the "natural" level, depending on the amount of snowmelt within the Tahoe Basin and the flow released downstream. Since 1871 the river's volume has usually depended on the amount of water allowed to pass through the dam.

Von Schmidt's daring scheme worried Nevadans for 35 years. He had all the legal authority necessary from California officials to rechannel the water to the San Francisco area. At times he seemed to have enough capital to do so. But the technical problems of lifting the water across the mountains to the west and pumping it across the Central Valley were beyond his capability, fortunately for Nevada and the future of the lake.

These prospects did not discourage the growth of small industrial works along the channel of the river in California, before it reaches the Nevada state line. Because the Central Pacific Railroad laid its tracks down the canyon in the 1860s, small industries followed. Lumber and flour mills, mining and milling operations, a furniture factory, and ice ponds all came and went, leaving a residue of pollutants. But most of these endeavors were modest in scale, and their impact seems to have been temporary.

On the California side of the border, the Truckee's flow is supplemented by input from several small streams and enhanced by reservoirs created over the decades for storage and flood control— Donner and Independence lakes and the reservoirs at Martis, Prosser, Stampede, and Boca. All these were controversial dams, intended to deal with flood and drought, but they became part of the river's growing obligation.

In spite of its tortured history, the upper Truckee remains one of the preferred attractions in eastern California and western Nevada. The comments of Samuel G. Houghton about its western canyon in 1975 were still generally accurate a quarter century later: "People should be thankful for the consequence of an unspoiled canyon. There are no rows of rockpiles left from vanished dredges, no landscapes torn and wasted by hydraulic mining. A few intruding enterprises came and went, like the river-polluting paper mill at Floriston, the brewery at Boca, and all the ice houses that flourished along that part of the Truckee during the early days of railroading" (64–65).

As the river flows eastward, it crosses the Truckee Meadows where Reno, Sparks, and their suburbs sprouted on the high sagebrush plain. In this benign natural bowl, where the Donner party rested in the autumn of 1846 before climbing upward to disaster in the canyon, the river offered an interval of relaxation. The meadows were largely undisturbed, their grasses and fishery available for those who had the patience and skills required for survival. The Washo bands found sustenance there for generations. The Donner party was the final group of Anglo-European innocents on this path. Their history gave notoriety to the Truckee River that echoed for decades.

Only twenty years after the Donner group passed this way, the steam-powered engines of the Central Pacific Railroad approached from the west. The Great Basin enclave was punctured by the industrial revolution in the Truckee Meadows. It was the gift of the river that invited the railroad barons to establish Reno in this semidesert bowl where the Truckee River emerges from the Sierra Nevada.

The early settlers coaxed the high desert terrain into fruitful production. With their aesthetic tastes they created a community of tree worshipers, "The City of Trembling Leaves" in the affectionate description of Walter Van Tilburg Clark. The pioneers diverted the river onto the hundred square miles of sagebrush terrain over which Reno expanded during the next century. A growing network of irrigation ditches encouraged dairies, ranches, and orchards. They enabled a traditional "city"—a commercial marketplace more stable than the rocky, rowdy mining camps in the nearby mountains—to establish roots. The aorta of the river distributed its fluid through arteries to various corners of the Truckee Meadows.

As the years passed and the little city evolved into a tourist destination, it tended to be gentle to the flowing water. At times residents dumped refuse or neglected the sewage plant; urban trash often threatened. But in the long term the Truckee suffered little damage in the context of the urban growth in the Meadows. As late as the 1950s the river still flowed through Reno with minor pollution. In the 1990s and 2000s Reno's municipal planners made a noble effort to restore and enhance the river's beauty after decades of neglect.

But downriver, east of Reno, the scenario changes. The canyon is more constricted; the river is more vulnerable, becoming narrower at the Truckee reefs. It shares its diminished scope with the railroad and those determined to divert the water to "beneficial use" on some of the most parched terrain of western Nevada.

Soon after the turn of the century, the concept of Congressman Newlands became law. In 1905 the federal government built Derby Dam, twenty-five miles east of Reno, to divert more than half the Truckee water from the main channel toward the Carson River. Thereafter, the lower Truckee and Pyramid Lake were left with a greatly diminished flow. The Truckee thus was summoned early in the twentieth century to do double duty, to serve two rival downstream needs—those of the Pyramid Lake Paiutes and the Newlands Project. Let us return to our narrative about the Carson River, which we dammed up a few pages back.

Newlands and His Project

Congressman Newlands had the legislative skill to write into federal law a concept called "reclamation" and to apply it to Nevada. On the Carson and Truckee rivers the result was less a matter of *reclaiming* land for agriculture than *imposing* a totally different ecosystem on some of the least-promising acreage in the West. The initial dream (or scheme) assumed that 400,000 acres could be cultivated near the sink of the Carson River in western Nevada on a patch of the driest terrain. (This plan was born when other parts of the agrarian West were already producing grains and other foodstuffs for which there were no ready markets.)

This project involved building not only Derby Dam and the thirty-one-mile long Truckee Canal to divert the flow toward the

Carson River. More important was construction of a larger second dam in the Carson channel to impound waters for agrarian use and for an electrical power plant. Lahontan Reservoir, completed in 1915, was designed to hold 300,000 acre-feet of water from the rivers as an insurance policy against years of drought. Congress created the Truckee-Carson Irrigation District to manage the water under the supervision of the U.S. Bureau of Reclamation.

When Congress funded the Newlands plan, it provided that this investment would eventually be repaid by the users (and it was). This made the program more politically palatable to skeptics when it was enacted. More important, this legislation set a precedent for pork-barrel projects at the federal level, and it brought decades of unforeseen litigation.

The Newlands legislation stimulated at least two differing schools of thought about water use that became more polarized as the years passed. One faction—probably the larger—saw diversion of Truckee and Carson waters onto once unproductive land through five hundred miles of canals as a positive and constructive innovation. The law provided that water would be made available to farms of no more than 160 acres. Most Nevadans took the view that Newlands (who became a senator in 1903) was a heroic champion of the little man, helping with the age-old mission of conquering and improving the land for human use on a small scale. Historians, following the paper trail, tended to embrace this creed. John Townley summarized this attitude in his book *Turn This Water Into Gold*, a metaphor describing the attitude of the hundreds of settlers who built the new towns of Fernley and Fallon. Fields of alfalfa and melons, fine dairies, and poultry farms seemed at first to validate federal and individual investments.

Opponents of the plan were more fractured and slower to formulate their messages, because the consequences did not appear for decades. The first to raise their voices in an articulate manner were ranchers in the upstream Carson Basin. They believed river water that was rightfully theirs had been stolen by an aggressive federal government for the benefit of downstream property owners—among whom Newlands was a prominent figure. Litigation plodded on for decades, but ultimately downstream users in Churchill and Lyon counties prevailed with most of their "rights" intact. Waters of the commingled rivers were devoted primarily to the purposes that Congressman Newlands intended.

In the long run, the transfer of the Truckee waters onto the arid land around Fernley and Fallon produced unforeseen economic problems. Markets for the melons and turkeys produced there were far away and the supply of water variable, in spite of the network of dams and canals. Whereas the original scheme assumed that 400,000 acres would be cultivated, in fact no more than 87,500 acres could actually be put into production with the available water. The alkaline-heavy soil was more difficult to cultivate than anticipated. Farmers were accused of chronic waste of water.

Other parts of the basin also felt the impact. The Stillwater Wildlife Management Area, located a dozen miles northeast of Fallon, has two small bodies of water, formerly fed by the Carson River, resting places for migratory birds. Although shallow and seasonally variable, they are crucial to the ecosystem. Thousands of ducks and geese visit annually when the flow of water is adequate.

Later in the century, growing numbers of upstream and downstream critics found fault with the Newlands Project for various reasons. All this gave ammunition to environmentalists and Native Americans who spoke against the project. By midcentury, the wisdom of the Newlands scheme was a matter for debate. But by then thousands of settlers had made their homes on the reclaimed lands. And a few hundred Native Americans clung to their tribal lands on that other downstream branch of the Truckee—where the Pyramid Lake Paiute tribe had practiced its survival arts for generations.

Pyramid Lake: An Endangered Desert Jewel

When John C. Frémont and his fellow explorers first saw Pyramid Lake in 1844, they were dazzled by its azure brilliance in its bleak desert setting. Near the point where the river enters the lake, they dined on a banquet of fish, which they called "salmon-trout," later known as the "cutthroat."

European Americans of that era considered the wandering Native American tribes to be in need of "civilization," which meant developing and exploiting nature's resources. In 1859 federal Indian agent Frederick Dodge recommended that an "Indian farm" be established at this site (and also at Walker Lake), to enable the Natives to develop the skills of agriculture rather than the nomadic food-gathering practices of their ancestors. The federal government intended to train Indians to become farmers rather than foragers. In 1874 President U. S. Grant ratified this recommendation in an executive order, designating a strip of riverbank land along the lower Truckee canyon and a narrow zone around the lake for their use. The area resembled a misshapen tennis racket, with a narrow handle and an oval paddle surrounding the lake.

The Pyramid Lake Indian Reservation began when the Comstock bonanza (1860s–1870s) was at its peak, as the Central Pacific was under construction, and when a town named Reno emerged in the Truckee Meadows (after 1868). New industries and settlements drastically changed the lives of the tribe and the fishery they relied on. Those who separately formed the reservation, constructed the railroad, and built the "tough little town on the Truckee" were working at cross-purposes, but they did not recognize the fact at the time.

During the eighty years after the first appearance of the Anglo-Americans, the Paiutes and newcomers fished the cutthroat trout almost to extinction. As passenger trains passed through the Truckee canyon, their mobile dining cars became a ready market for the fish, which were usually abundant at the mouth of the lake in winter and springtime. For decades, the railroad promoters and Paiutes were content with this arrangement. At times, newspapers reported that fewer fish were making their way upstream, and a few concerned citizens complained that the trout were disappearing. But with the help of commercial marketers, the Indians took as many from the mouth of the river as they could haul to the towns and railroad stations.

Several factors contributed to the decline in the trout population. Sawdust from upstream lumber mills, mostly in California, polluted the river bottom. Timber trash accumulated at the sluggish mouth of the river at Pyramid Lake, making it more difficult for the trout to swim upstream to spawn. Another obstruction was the so-called Indian Dam, constructed by the tribe near the mouth of the river to irrigate the best bottomlands on the Paiute Reservation. This formidable obstacle, originally built in 1871 and often "improved," stopped the trout as they tried to migrate. It also gave the Paiutes and their agents better opportunities to harvest the delicious fish for the market. The construction of Derby Dam farther upstream in 1905 to divert water for the Newlands Project was a relatively late development in the destruction of the Pyramid Lake fishery, which was endangered before the twentieth century began. The fishery was presumed dead by the late 1930s.

The federal government complicated the situation further with litigation. In 1914, when the Bureau of Reclamation wanted to learn how much unappropriated water remained in the river, it filed a "friendly lawsuit" to seek a court determination. This proceeding, widely know as the *Orr Ditch* case, involved all users of record of Truckee river water in Nevada, and it continued for more than thirty years. In 1944 a consent decree—which meant that nearly all litigants agreed—emerged from the court. This presumably settled the issue once and for all according to the doctrine of prior appropriation.

Yet the issue would not die. Another storm of litigation hit the courts again in the 1960s as population pressures on the Truckee Basin grew. The federal government, whose attorneys had pressed for settlement in the 1930s and 1940s, revived the *Orr Ditch* case in 1974 on the grounds that the rights of the Paiutes to a fishery had not been adequately considered in the first trial. This "new" case dragged on for yet another decade, until resolved in the U.S. Supreme Court in 1983. The Court affirmed that the settlement made in 1944 remained valid. Even then, conflicting claims about the different rights of California and Nevada were not resolved, spilling over into disputes in the Carson and Walker watersheds and on the upper Truckee in California.

Through most of its history, the Pyramid Reservation was home to only a few hundred people; fluctuations in population have been small, and the Native Americans remaining on the reservation have usually endured a level of poverty far beneath their upstream neighbors. In the late twentieth century they sought to benefit from a potential tourist business, encouraged by the stunning beauty of their azure desert lake and an attractive museum.

For many years Senator Harry Reid of Nevada sought to refine the remaining difference on the use of the precious, finite supply of water in the Truckee Basin. The senator's efforts reflected a dedicated commitment to environmental concerns, the needs of farmers, and the rights of the Native Americans. His efforts had considerable success, but in view of the long, tortured history of the waterway, one could not confidently predict that the matter has been permanently settled.

Walker River and Lake: Poverty, Weaponry, Slow Death

The Walker Basin is the weakest, most vulnerable sibling in the triad of rivers that have their origins along the eastern crest of the Sierra Nevada. The 160 miles of its course offered few incentives to emigrants, farmers, and early miners. The routes through the Sierra Nevada to California in this region are less accessible, the grass along its banks more sparse, and the mineral prospects less promising than those in the Carson and Truckee river basins.

California cattlemen claimed the promising grazing lands in Smith and Mason valleys as early as the 1850s and began building homes in the '60s. Crop cultivation and hay production became the primary industries, requiring diversion of the river's flow onto the arid lands. As the upstream population grew, the amount of water flowing into Walker Lake diminished. In northern Mason Valley, near Yerington, the two forks of the river converge, providing a rare opportunity for farming and ranching.

The lowest lands on the Walker River and the lake became an Indian reservation in 1859–1874 by the same process that applied to the Truckee-Pyramid Basin. Here, as in the case of the Truckee, Indian agents tried to encourage an agrarian community among the Native Americans with only modest success. The Paiute community on the lower Walker River fared marginally better than its northern sibling because the population pressures were fewer, no upstream sawmills polluted the channel, and no transcontinental railroad passed its way. But the Walker is a much smaller stream with only about half the flow of the Truckee, with few suitable places for upstream storage.

At the south end of Walker Lake, Hawthorne emerged as a hard-scrabble town in 1881. Established as a distribution point by the Carson & Colorado Railroad, it failed to prosper because it did not enjoy most of the assets of its northern neighbors—nearby mining booms, pasturelands, and proximity to the main commercial routes. However, it served briefly as a county seat and a minor distribution center and thus survived for the next fifty years. Eventually, in the 1930s Hawthorne was selected as the site of a U.S. Navy ammunition depot—a facility unwanted in more populous parts of the nation because of the dangers involved in processing and storing its highly explosive inventory. (We will discuss the ammunition depot in the next chapter.)

Because of upstream diversions, especially in Smith and Mason valleys, Walker Lake has had a "water deficit" for most of the past 125 years. State officials and local lake watchers have been aware for decades that this resource is slowly dying. The indigenous cut-throat trout are no longer able to spawn, and the rising level of salt makes other life forms less viable. Lamentations are frequent, but no solutions to the problem are evident, and pollution from the ammunition dump is yet to be resolved.

The gloomy fate of the lake may not be entirely due to upstream diversions. Scientists who served the Nevada Division of Water Planning in the 1990s concluded that at least twice in the past 5,000 years, Walker Lake has disappeared because the climate has not provided enough moisture to sustain it. Wet and dry cycles are the norm in the Great Basin. The contemporary era has been mostly dry, and the upstream diversions are accelerating nature's cruel agenda.

The Humboldt: Travel and Pollution

The Humboldt River is the wayward cousin of northern Nevada's river family. It flows the wrong way—from northeast to southwest—unlike its three companions, which emerge from the Sierra Nevada and proceed northeastward. These four streams seem to be trying to meet and blend their waters, as they did thousands of years ago in ancient Lake Lahontan. Only rarely, in recent times of flooding, have the waters of the Humboldt and the Carson merged at a low ridge between Fallon and Lovelock.

The sluggish Humboldt River slithers across the Great Basin for a thousand miles, but it crosses only three hundred miles from its sources to the Humboldt Sink. In wet years (as in 2005), it moves like a fast serpent, rushing toward its destination. In dry years (as in 2001–2004), it slinks almost motionless toward its natural inland resting place. Here it provides a sanctuary for migratory birds, when the upstream sources and the seasons allow.

This centuries-old process is endangered. The upriver gold mines in recent years have pumped vast amounts of water from their pits into the upper Humboldt, inducing greater than normal flow in the channel. In doing so, these gold miners have drawn down the natural water table in the upper Humboldt Basin by an amount that hydrologists are trying to ascertain. "Dewatering" the upstream pits may temporarily enhance but eventually restrict or poison the future flow of the lower Humboldt.

In the late 1990s a vigorous debate raged between mining companies and environmentalists about the long-term effects of pumping down the subterranean waters for the benefit of the gold producers upstream. According to some calculations, it will take more than two hundred years to replenish the aquifer beneath the upper Humboldt Basin. In the meantime, the artificial lakes that remain after the mines have closed will remain toxic for an uncertain period of time. Mine owners and their spokesmen offer assurances that any damage will be minimal, temporary, and within the limits defined by current standards. Environmentalists argue that the laws now in effect to ensure cleanup after the mining and processing are finished are not adequate to compensate for the damage done.

Drought and Flood: Capricious Nature

It may seem as though the Truckee and Carson rivers are predictable creatures, capable of being domesticated for the uses of civilization. Generally, this has been the case, but at times nature ignores the "improvements" humans have imposed, and global warming may have changed the rules.

The Truckee River may serve as an example. It has reached flood stage in the Meadows at least fourteen times since 1860—on the average of once every decade. Some of these deluges have been devastating to property. One recent memorable event was the so-called New Year's flood of 1997, which did damage estimated at more than six hundred million dollars on the Carson and Truckee rivers. The upstream storage capacity built in the past century has proved inadequate when melting rain falls on a wet snowpack and the soil is saturated. At such times the torrents carry all before them in a muddy surge. Human memories are short, and nature takes its revenge with little warning.

On the other hand, the dry cycles can leave the riverbeds parched, the thirsty upstream users having soaked up every trickle that can be coaxed from the fragile ribbons of moisture. Severe water shortages occurred in 1928–1937, 1953–1955, and 1976–1977 in the most populous areas of the state. A period of drought occurred throughout the region in 1987–1994; another was under way in the early 2000s. Nevadans have often known spans of years when the existing water "rights" could not be honored. At these times, when the technology is available, utility companies and private users try to lift even more from underground aquifers to supply the needs of a constantly growing population.

We need a last word on Pyramid Lake. In an average year more water evaporates from its surface than flows into it, so its level has dropped about eighty feet since Frémont first saw it 160 years ago. Although some upstream storage has been enhanced and government policies have often tried to slow the process, Pyramid Lake may eventually be destined for the same sad fate that its sibling—Walker Lake—has suffered.

CHAPTER FOUR

The Southern Waters

In Las Vegas Valley the phrase "liquid gold" means neither oil nor money; it suggests water. In the twentieth century Las Vegas became one of the least-probable urban centers in the United States, located in one of the driest, hottest spots on the continent. During the past century, it evolved from being a small watering hole in a parched, dusty southwestern valley into an extravagant tourist destination, envied and imitated across the globe. Its population grew from 30 residents in 1900 to more than 1.5 million a hundred years later. Its decorative water fountains throw colorful jets into the desert air day and night. The massive interstate highway network and McCarran International Airport bring tens of millions of visitors to the Las Vegas region every year. In 2005 McCarran was the sixth busiest airport in America in terms of passenger traffic, far ahead of many other far larger cities. It claimed several of the largest hotels in the world.

Judged by the commercial standards of the twentieth century, Las Vegas has been a stunning success. It sets the standard for compulsive, indulgent entertainment. Its main "industry"—tourism—usually reports profits even in times of recession. The ecological consequences have been little studied until recently.

Since the days when the earliest Hispanic explorers identified the oasis they called *las vegas* (the meadows), water has been the crucial factor in defining human activity in the valley. The Mormon missionaries, nineteenth-century ranchers, even millionaire senator William Clark who built the railroad between Salt Lake City and Los Angeles across the valley in 1904–1905 could not have undertaken their experiments had it not been for the artesian springs that oozed forth in the middle of this bleak basin. For the first four decades after 1905, Las Vegans gulped the natural sources of surface water and enhanced the natural springs with artesian wells. Agents of Senator Clark, in laying out the town only a century ago, installed a network of wooden pipes along its streets. He arranged for an icehouse near the railroad station to refresh the trains passing through. Clark's Las Vegas Land & Water Company managed the water distribution system for the next fifty years. As the wartime boom of the 1940s began, these facilities were not adequate for the expanding community. The water company became a feudal relic, retarding the development of the municipality.

Searching for a Water Policy

For four decades, as Las Vegas grew, its civic leaders lurched toward urban status without a coherent plan. From the beginning, Las Vegans were extravagant in using the available resources from local springs and wells. The consumption per person was much higher than in most American cities, even in the desert Southwest—maybe because it was hot or maybe because Las Vegans had become accustomed to a relatively generous supply from those almost miraculous sources in the middle of the arid desert.

Businesses, residents, and visitors alike used quantities that hydrologists knew to be excessive. By 1939 more than five hundred wells were pumping from the aquifer; the water table was falling rapidly. In that year state engineer Alfred Merritt Smith persuaded the Nevada legislature to enact a law authorizing the state to regulate pumping from subsurface sources. Under his leadership, the

state government adopted a responsible water management policy with restrictions that well served the growing city for another
thirty years.

The primary hopes of the city for a long-term source of water
rested on the great river that flowed just beyond the horizon a
few miles to the east. Under the provisions of the Colorado River
Compact approved by Congress in 1922 and later adjusted by the
courts, Nevada was entitled to draw three hundred thousand acre-
feet annually from the river, or about 2 percent of its anticipated
flow. Reaching this settlement was a long, tortured process. Nevada held few cards in this complicated poker game. The Colorado
River system flows through or adjacent to seven states—Wyoming,
Colorado, New Mexico, Utah, Arizona, Nevada, and California—all
of which had to ratify the compact. (Mexico was also acknowledged
to have a claim, but pragmatic Americans gave little attention to
that fact.) The river system was presumed to carry an average of
fifteen million acre-feet per year (AFY) for use in the United States.
This figure proved to be too optimistic in the long run, and decades
of hard-fought litigation followed in the federal courts. The 1922
compact paved the way for Congress to authorize the construction
of Boulder (later Hoover) Dam in Black Canyon on the Nevada-
Arizona border. This project lubricated much of the Southwest
with its most essential lifeline.

Hoover (Boulder) Dam

The construction of Boulder Dam in less than five years in the early
1930s was a magnificent achievement, reminiscent of the building
of the transcontinental railroad sixty years earlier. The 726-foot-
high wedge of concrete poured into a canyon gorge—with its huge
turbines for generating electricity and its ability to tame a wild
river—was regarded as a wonder of the modern world. At the peak
of construction, five thousand men were employed, and a nearby
desert plateau was transformed into the oasis of Boulder City. This
community became a model for the arid Southwest, showing how

the diversion of the river could bring greenery to much of Arizona and southern California.

After the completion of the dam, Lake Mead began to rise behind it. Nevada's three hundred thousand AFY was legally, but not physically, available. An elaborate network of pumps and pipes would be required to lift the water into Las Vegas Valley, but the cost of building a pipeline across or through the mountains was beyond the budget of a city of fewer than ten thousand people or even a state of a hundred thousand. Federal help was essential.

The first steps in this process came in the early 1940s when a federal defense appropriation mandated the construction of a pipeline to serve the Basic Magnesium plant south of Las Vegas (see chapter 2). Because of the wartime need for the rare metal, the national treasury did what Las Vegas could not do for itself: piped and pumped water from the lake into Las Vegas Valley. After the defense needs had been met and much of the Basic complex was adapted to other uses, more of this flow became available to local communities. The Nevada legislature enabled Las Vegas to form a public water district in 1947, thus allowing the city to wean itself from its dependency on the private company established by Senator Clark four decades earlier.

Another crucial turning point came in 1954. The privately owned Las Vegas Land & Water Company, facing mounting problems in maintaining its system, sold its interests to the new publicly owned Las Vegas Valley Water District (LVVWD), which began more systematic planning for future needs. By the summer of 1955 the pipeline pumping water from Lake Mead to Henderson was extended into Las Vegas. Yet this was only a quick fix in view of the rapid growth of the communities.

The Southern Nevada Water Project, 1954–1990s

Senator Alan Bible (1954–1975) provided the legislative muscle to obtain the federal funding needed to bring more Colorado River water into Las Vegas Valley. As a former state attorney general who had argued Nevada's case in the complicated interstate water litigation, Bible took to Washington a keen appreciation of the needs in Las Vegas Valley. He guided administrative planning at the local and federal levels and managed the legislation that authorized and appropriated funds for the project. His personal friendships with Presidents John F. Kennedy and Lyndon B. Johnson were crucial when Nevada's interests became entangled in prolonged litigation over the river. Bible had support from Senator Howard Cannon (1959–1982), whose relations with the White House were also good. Despite the weakness of Nevada's lone member of the House of Representatives, Congressman Walter Baring, a consistent anti-environmentalist, the senators were able to secure money for the project in October 1965.

The Southern Nevada Water Project proceeded in stages. A tunnel through the mountains and a sprawling complex of pipelines did the job that Nevada never could have accomplished on its own. The first phase pumped 130,000 acre-feet per year into Las Vegas by 1971. The second and third stages, completed in 1982, delivered most of the remainder of Nevada's allotted water entitlement to Las Vegas Valley. The large pumping station and distribution complex cost more than a half-billion dollars, funded primarily from state bonds and a federal loan. By the 1990s about 80 percent of Las Vegas's water was coming from the Colorado River.

Even this huge hydraulic network provided only a temporary solution to the growing metropolitan needs. The river is over-allocated, that is, more water has been granted to the various users by agreements and court decrees than the long-range flow patterns of the river will justify. As the valley's population rose from about 450,000 in 1980 to 750,000 in 1990 and 1.2 million in 2000, Las Vegas Valley Water District planners estimated that at the current level of growth and the same patterns of usage, they would be unable to meet the area's requirements beyond about 2010. In the 1990s Las Vegas Valley users were consuming 316 gallons of water per capita per day, as compared with 281 in Reno, 209 in Phoenix, and 158 in Tucson (NDEP, *Quality of the Environment Report*).

But nature had a different agenda that threatened to choke southern Nevada's penchant for expansion. The entire region has experienced two long droughts in the past two decades. Between 1985 and 1993 the water level in Lake Mead dropped almost every year. The continuing downward trend worried hydrological planners. Runoff improved between 1993 and 1997; in 1998 the level of the lake was near the highest point in history. Yet state meteorologists and environmental scientists warned that the entire region might be vulnerable to a prolonged era of diminishing rain and snow in the mountains.

Expansion of the treatment plant and pipelines into Las Vegas Valley proceeded into the twenty-first century, but the expansion of Clark County's population outpaced the improvement. At the end of the 1990s, drought conditions recurred, and by 2006 Lake Mead had dropped to its lowest level since 1968.

Massive Imports from the North? 1990s–2007

The uncertainty of the Colorado River source caused LVVWD planners to look northward into Lincoln, Nye, and White Pine counties, three thinly populated rural areas where additional natural watersheds could be found and where large underground aquifers were believed to exist. In 1989 the water district proposed a $1.5 billion project that would involve drilling 140 deep wells and building scores of new reservoirs in the northern counties. These sources would then be connected to Las Vegas by 1,000 miles of pipelines, a scheme much more ambitious than the Southern Nevada Water Project, but with a much smaller resource actually in sight. LVVWD managers applied for water rights from the state engineer as a preliminary step toward this goal. The objective would be to divert some two hundred thousand acre-feet of water to Las Vegas each year. LVVWD spokesmen referred to this as the Cooperative Water Project.

Nonprofit public-service groups dedicated to protecting the environment quickly responded. Such a massive project, they argued, would do untold damage to plants, wildlife, and existing human uses of the land and water in a region that includes more than one-third of Nevada. The consequences would be felt as far north as Ely and the Great Basin National Park, more than 250 miles away. The plan also caused alarm in adjacent regions of California, especially in Death Valley, where a delicate desert ecosystem relies on underground water that might be depleted if such a massive complex of wells were created.

Whereas rural Nevadans and environmentalists argued that enormous ecological and social damage would occur in areas that were being "dewatered," Las Vegas planners countered with the claim that much of the water use in northern Nevada is wasteful and uneconomical. About 90 percent of Nevada's developed water in the northern counties is used for irrigation. Yet the crops produced account for only a small fraction of the state's economy. The water can be put to more "beneficial" use, LVVWD spokesmen asserted, in the commercial enterprises of Las Vegas than in the pastures and grazing lands up north. (The same kind of debate was under way in California, between farmers in the Imperial Valley and the coastal cities.) Both California and Nevada have vital economic interests in finding water for their growing urban areas; in fact, there is a political imperative to do so because of the growing domestic and commercial needs in a geographically arid region. The more rural northern regions have less influence on the decision-making processes as time goes on.

It had been relatively easy to tap the water of the Colorado River, so near to Las Vegas and seemingly so abundant; this kind of diversion of surface water has a history as old as the earliest recorded human civilizations in the Middle East. It is quite another matter to seek to plumb the deep aquifers of the delicate high deserts to the north, where both the quantity and the consequences are unknown.

One continuing question not answered early in the twenty-first century was the total cost of such a project. Independent researchers estimated in the 1990s that the plan might cost much more than the $1.5 billion originally predicted by the LVVWD. Guesses ranged upward to more than $4.4 billion for construction, and, depending on the method of financing, final costs could be as much as $7.5 billion. There was little doubt that the price Las Vegas users would pay for their water would increase severalfold if this alternative were selected.

To make the so-called Cooperative Water Project more palatable, the LVVWD launched a water conservation program in the Las Vegas area in the 1990s, adopting new building codes that required the installation of low-volume plumbing fixtures in newly constructed buildings and water reuse facilities for decorative water fountains, car washing services, and similar nonessential uses. The district also restructured its water rates for the purpose of encouraging conservation by its customers.

Late in 1993 Secretary of the Interior Bruce Babbitt (who had previously been a consultant to Nevada's smaller counties when they resisted the first LVVWD importation proposal) visited Las Vegas and promised to help find ways to bring more water to Las Vegas from other sources—possibly from neighboring states that might be willing to sell some of their allotted rights.

Also in 1993 the LVVWD asked the state engineer's office to postpone action on the applications for water rights in the rural counties to the north, as it concentrated its efforts instead on negotiating with water users in other states for additional rights to Colorado River water. Other ambitious importation schemes surfaced that autumn when the LVVWD met with the Colorado River Commission to consider nine different plans. These included the possibility of buying agricultural water rights from private interests in Arizona and California; acquiring rights to glaciers in Alaska, Canada, or the Columbia River; and building a desalination plant on the lower

Colorado River for Mexico in exchange for the right to use some of that country's allotted water from the Colorado.

The proposal to import water from the North lay dormant for ten years before it reappeared. In the meantime, the population of Clark County increased by nearly a million people. In the autumn of 2004, a more modest version of this scheme received approval in Washington when Nevada's congressional delegation reached a compromise in the U.S. Senate and House of Representatives. This measure, labeled the Lincoln County Conservation, Recreation, and Development Act, passed both houses. It won endorsement from the county commissioners of Lincoln County but met stiff resistance in White Pine County and among environmental groups. Some organizations concerned about the preservation of wilderness supported the measure. It was the first time in recent memory the environmental movement took different readings on their compass. The Lincoln County bill got rapid approval because it was packaged with provisions intended to stimulate economic development of the upland region whose economic base in mining and agriculture activities had faded.

Under the provisions of this law, the Southern Nevada Water Authority (snwa), an expanded version of the lvvwd, can draw as much as 200,000 acre-feet of water per year from the region, and it is granted a free right-of-way for 260 miles (which stretches northward into east-central Nevada) for transfer of the water southward. This will involve drilling for an uncertain aquifer and piping on a scale not previously known in Nevada. To sweeten the deal, the law provides that about 87,000 acres of land in Lincoln County can be offered for sale, with most of the funds to be divided between the county and the Bureau of Land Management (blm). The blm is expected to use the revenue for management and protection of archaeological resources and conservation. A small portion of the revenue from the anticipated land sales would go to the state education fund.

This cornucopia of presumed benefits seemed too attractive to ignore. Not only would it give the thirsty Las Vegas Valley another potential source of its most necessary elixir, but it would also provide benefits to Lincoln County, one of the poorest in the state. It would presumably strengthen the rural economy by offering some initiatives to make wilderness areas more accessible.

Nevada's lawmakers had made a Faustian bargain. Unknown large quantities of fluid wealth would be mined (in this case pumped) from underground sources to slake the thirst of Las Vegas. Las Vegas Valley could continue to expand, betting on the promise of a new liquid bonanza that would be siphoned southward from underground sources not only in Lincoln County but perhaps eventually from farther north and from Utah. Water managers in Utah were ringing alarm bells in 2005–2006. Water resources do not respect state boundaries.

The Virgin River

The LVVWD had plenty of initiative and skill even before it renewed its reach for water in the adjacent northern counties of Nevada. When its scheme for water from the northern counties was stalled in the early 1990s, the district sought and won rights in the Virgin River tributary to the Colorado. In 1994 the state engineer's office approved the water district's plan to acquire new rights from this source.

The headwaters of the Virgin "River" rise in southern Utah northeast of the Dixie National Forest. The stream flows through the northwestern corner of Arizona before reaching Nevada, where it supplied essential irrigation for the Mormon villages of Mesquite and Bunkerville for more than a century. Las Vegas water planners prudently proposed a point downstream from all others who had existing water rights for their diversion. They made a successful case to the state engineer that they were taking for Las Vegas only unappropriated water, thus doing no harm to existing rights. Yet other environmental reports indicated that the Virgin was an endangered river.

Privatization: The New Water-Witching

During the frantic maneuvering for new water sources in the early 1990s, one promoter, like the fabled water witches of old desert stories, even promised to reveal the source of a secret subterranean aquifer—the location was known only to himself—if a generous finder's fee were guaranteed to him. The water authorities of Las Vegas Valley were not ready to place a bet on such a dubious proposition, but they were willing to gamble with a form of "privatization" of their future water sources.

The southern Nevada water tangle is a local example of a global problem. The urbanized world is running short of fresh, clean water. The World Bank has estimated that throughout the globe, the existing supplies will be exhausted by 2025. As governments are downsizing and turning their traditional duties over to private interests, its allocation is being placed in the hands of for-profit corporations. In southern Nevada, the private interest manager manipulating the enterprise is the Vidler Water Company, a private entrepreneur interlocked with one of the largest private landowners in Nevada. Its agents formed a partnership with the local government of Lincoln County (one of the largest and poorest local jurisdictions in the state) to manage the transaction. The water resources of the region are thus in the clutches of a for-profit company.

And in the intricate labyrinth of ecology, we must return to the minerals-processing industry that we discussed earlier. Water and land are complementary resources, and events that occurred on the ground a half century ago may be affecting the contemporary water supply.

The Perchlorate Problem

Land and water problems from the past and present are intricately intertwined. Although most of the water consumed in Las Vegas Valley now comes from Lake Mead by way of the Southern Nevada Water Project, groundwater is still important in many ways. The aquifer that supplied the pumps a century ago still serves, and its subterranean waters still flow toward the lake.

As detailed in chapter 2, in Basic-Henderson sixty years ago much toxic waste from the BMI was dumped onto the ground. In later years, successor corporations that used the facilities continued to dump refuse on the desert. One of the deadly chemicals used to create rocket fuel and fertilizer was perchlorate, a substance that can interfere with thyroid function in the human body. This chemical was identified in the Las Vegas Wash and Lake Mead in 1997. At that time no standard existed for the amount of this contaminant that could be allowed in drinking water, but it was known to be dangerous. Perchlorate was produced at Henderson from 1945 until 1998, including at the PEPCON factory until it was destroyed by the explosion of 1988. After the substance was discovered in Lake Mead and its urban tributary in 1997, the EPA, NDEP, SNWA, and private interests formed a team to remove and filter the poisons as completely as possible.

The level of success is in the eye of the beholder. State and local authorities believed they were making substantial progress. Independent analysts remained uncertain. In the summer of 2005 studies were under way to determine whether more than two thousand homes might be built on some of the ground where perchlorate had been manufactured.

California's History Lesson

As Las Vegas water authorities pressed their search for additional sources of the West's most valuable resource, they could not avoid comparisons with the unfortunate record of southern California's experience. In 1906 cunning promoters arranged the aggressive exploitation of the water resources from that state's northern counties to move the flow southward, from the mountains into the desert. Ever since Los Angeles reached northward into the Owens Valley in the early 1900s to purchase appropriated rights, the water distribution system has been controversial. In the 1970s a bitter struggle erupted between the thirsty, urbanized southland on the one hand and the advocates of the northern counties and the environmental movement on the other. The environmentalists mounted a growing effort that increased in strength through the 1980s and won some major victories in the state courts, blocking the continuing exploitation of northern water resources and requiring assessments of damage to the ecological systems. Los Angeles incurred much adverse publicity across the nation, especially in its struggle to maintain high levels of water usage from Mono Lake, some three hundred miles to the north, in spite of evidence that a delicate natural resource was being destroyed. Ultimately, a combination of court decisions and legislation forced the metropolis to scale back its water usage from Mono Lake.

As Norris Hundley Jr. wrote in his 1992 book, *The Great Thirst*, "That Californians—and the nation, for that matter—have abused the land and waterscape and failed to develop a coherent water policy hardly seems surprising for a people with a centuries-old exploitive tradition and with a (perhaps illogical) desire to accommodate growth with environmental restoration and at least some wilderness preservation" (421). Southern Nevada developers and politicians were treading the same path in environmental matters as their neighbors had done earlier; whether they would learn from that neighbor in time to avoid further ecological damage was a rhetorical question.

Davis Dam

Nevada shares another dam with Arizona at the most southern tip of the state. The federal government began work on yet another reclamation project sixty-seven miles south of Hoover Dam in 1942, which also stimulated the growth of Las Vegas. The purpose of Davis Dam was to generate additional electrical energy for the booming Southwest and to impound water eventually intended for Mexico under a 1944 treaty. This facility was named for Arthur Powell Davis, one of the early hydrological planners in the U.S. Reclamation Service.

Soon after construction began it was suspended, because man-power and materials were more urgently needed for World War II defense industries. The building of an earth-and-rock-filled dam resumed in 1946 and was completed five years later. Lake Mohave formed upstream from the dam, stretching almost the entire distance northward to the base of Hoover Dam. South of Davis Dam on a wide spot on the riverbank the resort town of Laughlin emerged during the 1980s, with several casinos and hotels to serve the growing throngs of tourists. This was yet another example of commercial progress at an unknown ecological cost.

A Microcosm

In its almost desperate quest for water, Las Vegas is a microcosm of the planet. In hundreds of places around the world, cities are reaching outward for new sources, often recklessly and without regard for the environmental consequences of their developments. On one level, this appears to be an overstatement, because the Water Resources Division of the state engineer's office has demonstrated high competence and energy in dealing with regional water problems. In its ruling on the application for Virgin River water, for example, the state engineer's office found that the LVVWD had adopted strict regulations against waste, with its "awareness patrol" and "home water survey" to encourage conservation. Yet it was also true that southern Nevada's growth had severely taxed the skills of its water-planning experts and that skepticism remained about the willingness of southern Nevada to make long-term commitments to conservation.

Westerners have typically told the story of the building of Hoover Dam and other reclamation projects in terms of human rationality—harnessing wild rivers and turning untamed forces into useful energy. Environmental historian Donald Worster understands this phenomenon differently. When it was being built in the 1930s, Boulder Dam was one of most remarkable structures of its kind in the world, a symbol of modern society's

ability to conquer nature and put its potential power to "beneficial" use. But Worster concludes that the later results were quite
unexpected. Hoover and Davis dams and a myriad of similar technological wonders became vast instruments for enabling small
groups of bureaucrats to administer the lives of others (210–12).
Worster chides those who admire the dam and fail to consider its
broader human and social implications. The builders of the dam
and the chorus of admirers ignored the fact that this and other so-
called reclamation improvements along the Colorado River caused
massive environmental damage to the major water resource of the
Southwest. They have also empowered giant California agribusi-
nesses and glitzy Nevada casino magnates.

The waters that have been transferred into Las Vegas Valley from
Lake Mead have also made possible the sprawling urban areas of
Las Vegas, Henderson, and their satellites. All the way from Sun-
rise Mountain in the Northeast to the slopes of Mount Charleston
in the Northwest to the uplands of Black Mountain in the South,
the urban presence is being felt in formerly uninhabited areas. But
the supply from the Colorado River has become more problematic
each year. And the water must be taken to these outlying areas;
often, developers encounter hard clay as they install the pipelines.
The city is conquering the desert in ways not contemplated only
a few decades ago. In the meantime, much of the valley floor has
subsided—dropping in places by as much as five feet—as subsurface water has been lifted to serve a thirsty population.

The diminished amount of Colorado River water reflects a
global problem on a regional scale. As Fred Pearce demonstrates
in his compelling book *When the Rivers Run Dry: Water—the Defining
Crisis of the Twenty-first Century*, "The Colorado is both legally and
hydrologically one of the most regulated rivers in the world. But
it is becoming clear that the legal and the hydrological no longer
mesh" (196).

McCarran International Airport in Las Vegas is another example
of the syndrome. In 1950 it was a remote rural landing place on the

outskirts of the small desert oasis. By 2005 it was the sixth busiest airport in the United States. An efficiently managed transportation hub, it serves the booming city and its worldwide clientele. It is a graphic example of how Nevada, the nation, and the world have challenged the ecosystem.

A herd of sheep grazing on the public domain. Note the barren landscape, a result of overgrazing. Photo by Jack Hursh.

Wild horses at Palomino Valley Wild Horse and Burro Placement Center near Reno. These animals were gathered from the public domain by the Bureau of Land Management to prevent their starvation. Many are rehabilitated and placed for adoption. Photo by Becky Purky, Bureau of Land Management.

Rangeland charred by fire in Elko County, 2006. Photo by Jack Hursh.

Lumber mill in the Sierra Nevada. Note the flume that carried logs from the mountain to the mill. Photo courtesy of R. J. Waters.

Lumber mill at Spooner's Summit in the Sierra Nevada, 1876. This timber was harvested for construction of the Comstock mines. Note the clear-cut slopes of the mountain, a cause of subsequent erosion. Photo courtesy of the Nevada Historical Society.

Extensive mine tailings at the Combination Mine dump near Virginia City. After more than a century, the tailings are still almost barren of vegetation. Photo by Kris Ann Pizarro.

Contemporary aerial view of Virginia City, looking west. The light-colored patches scattered below and above the town are mine tailings. Photo courtesy of the Nevada Bureau of Mines and Geology.

Charcoal ovens, or "beehives," near Pioche, built for converting local trees into charcoal for smelting ore. Photo by Kris Ann Pizarro.

Early view of the Basic Magnesium plant at Henderson. Photo courtesy of Special Collections, Lied Library, University of Nevada, Las Vegas.

A new scar on the land. A contemporary open pit mine in northern Nevada. There are several such mines in Nevada, most intended for the extraction of microscopic gold. Photo by Chris Ross, Bureau of Land Management.

An oil-pumping rig in Railroad Valley, eastern Nevada. Photo by Chris Ross, Bureau of Land Management.

The Brunswick Mill on the Carson River. Because of the enormous quantity of mercury released by the mill into the Carson River, this is Nevada's only federal "superfund" reclamation site. Photo courtesy of the W. M. Keck Museum, Mackay School of Mines, University of Nevada, Reno.

Evidence of land subsidence caused by
extensive pumping of underground water
in the Las Vegas Valley. Photo by John Bell.

BELOW: Deep fissures in the earth
reflecting land subsidence near Las Vegas.
In this case, the subsidence destroyed a
residential structure. Photo by John Bell.

Aerial view of Hoover Dam and Lake Mead. Photo courtesy of Special Collections, Lied Library, University of Nevada, Las Vegas.

Aerial view of the Las Vegas Airport (later McCarran International Airport) in 1950. Downtown Las Vegas can be seen in the distant background. Photo courtesy of the Clark County Department of Aviation.

Aerial view of McCarran International Airport, 2006. Heavy development completely surrounds the airport. Photo courtesy of the Clark County Department of Aviation.

Billboard target at Fallon Naval Air Station, 1960. Note scattered weapon debris in foreground. Photo courtesy of the U.S. Navy.

Using a dosimeter to check radioactive fallout on a Nevada ranch. Photo courtesy of the Atomic Testing Museum, Las Vegas.

Soldiers in training near an atomic bomb explosion at the Nevada Test Site, 1950s. Photo courtesy of the Atomic Testing Museum, Las Vegas.

View of Reno with Peavine Mountain in the background. Development is gradually consuming the lower slopes of this and other mountains surrounding Reno, closing off recreational trailheads and intruding into the habitat of native mule deer and other wildlife. Photo by Jack Hursh.

Dredging the Truckee River east of Reno to restore its natural channel. The Nature Conservancy is restoring a large tract of land in this area to provide habitat for wildlife and a natural floodplain for the river. Photo courtesy of the *Reno Gazette-Journal*.

CHAPTER FIVE

The Military Invasion

We need a deep immersion in art and history to realize how unmilitary, nonbellicose the United States was in 1940–1941, when war was raging in Europe and Asia. Before December 7 America was asleep, not only at Pearl Harbor. Nevada was widely perceived to be still a frontier land in the twilight of an era of mining booms, with a population density of one person per square mile. Our parents remembered World War I, which had been fought in distant lands with small impact on our then forty-eight states.

The attack of December 1941 awakened the drowsy nation like a fire alarm in the night. It was the 9/11 surprise of sixty-eight years ago. In the beginning, the government worried about a potential assault by the Japanese on the California coast, where most of the major military installations in the Far West were located dangerously near the Pacific Ocean. The military services had few inland bases. Nevada, with its abundance of uncommitted, government-owned land, became a choice for a second line of defense and a site for long-range preparation for future wars. Nevadans generally welcomed the advent of the new age of military preparedness. This attitude changed slowly as the years passed.

Fifty years later, by the 1990s, the military had claimed more than four million acres of Nevada land, mostly from the Bureau of Land Management but taking some of it from citizens by condemnation, purchase, or harassment. In addition, the armed forces had entered the airspace above the desert-and-range province, disturbing, with the roar of jet-powered engines, much of the sky above and the wilderness below.

Nellis Air Force Base

As the United States emerged from its posture of military weakness in 1941 to the world's superpower fifty years later, the transformation affected southern Nevada as much as any other region in America. Here the federal government created its largest internal air base and scattered the greatest junk pile of spent ammunition in North America.

The U.S. Army Air Corps acquired the field that eventually became Nellis Air Force Base just a few months before the attack on Pearl Harbor. At first the base served only as a gunnery school, which required the withdrawal of a sizable stretch of public domain desert, identified as the Las Vegas–Tonopah Bombing and Gunnery Range. During World War II and the Korean conflict, as Nellis became the primary fighter-plane training center in the U.S. military complex, the area needed for testing and training grew with little public attention. Nellis proudly identified itself as the "Home of the Fighter Pilot," the largest facility of its kind in the Western world.

As the United States became more deeply involved in the Vietnam conflict in the 1960s, military growth accelerated. The Las Vegas test range expanded to include an area larger than Connecticut—including more than 5 percent of the land within Nevada. The Tactical Air Command of the Air Force in 1966 established a "Weapons and Tactics Center" to meet the challenges of the latest war, selecting Nellis for its primary center. In a statement published in 1994, the air force reported that the base used more than 50 percent of the ammunition expended by the military branch. In addition to the aircraft assigned to the center's units, it served some of the training needs of friendly foreign governments.

Nevadans at first looked only at the income side of the ledger. From an employment level of approximately five thousand in the 1950s, the Nellis workforce expanded to more than nine thousand before the end of the 1960s. By 1989 Nellis had a payroll of twelve thousand, more than any other employer—public or private—in Las Vegas Valley. It generated more than a half-billion dollars annually in personal disposable income in Clark County. The prosperity from the expansion of Nellis coaxed most Nevadans into a promilitary posture in their public attitudes and expectations. Senator Howard Cannon, in 1958 the first Las Vegan ever elected to the U.S. Senate, gained a strategic seat on the Senate Armed Forces Committee. He gave consistent support to the air force's requests for funding projects in Nevada.

As southern Nevadans enjoyed the apparent economic benefits of the generous federal payroll, they virtually ignored a secondary fact: three million acres of the public domain had been reassigned to the U.S. Air Force. This change did not absolutely preclude other uses, but it greatly diminished them. Traditional uses for mining, grazing, wildlife habitat, and recreation were sharply curtailed. The growing public interest in clean air and pure water receded into an administrative twilight zone when military activities were involved. Concerns about environmental damage were seldom expressed. Nevada, a needy, undernourished sibling in the federal family, took what the federal government offered, but it knew nothing of the environmental bill that would come due later. It was a welfare patient in those years.

Through the 1980s the air force conducted secret tests of a new experimental military plane called "Stealth," with part of the activities at Nellis and part at the Tonopah Test Range, two hundred miles from Las Vegas. Because this operation was clandestine, it was difficult to assess the environmental impact. In a typical week hundreds rode buses from Nellis to the test range; the employment level for this operation at its peak was estimated to be twenty-five hundred. When air force representatives dumped the Stealth project in 1990, they could not estimate how many jobs would be lost in southern Nevada.

The most mysterious activities occurred at Groom Lake in the remote northeastern corner of the test site. The secrets surrounding this operation, occasionally mentioned in the national media, provided a cat-and-mouse game for curious speculators. The nature of these experiments and the ecological consequences may not be known for decades.

As the Cold War came to an end with the collapse of the Soviet bloc in 1989–1991, Nevada business interests felt unfamiliar shock waves. The air force deactivated a tactical fighter-plane unit at Nellis and removed many F-16s. The prospect that long-term reductions in the military-industrial complex would slim down a perennial source of growth was not a cheerful prospect for a city that had built its expectations for a half century on military expansion as well as tourism.

Did the downscaling of the military operations make any difference to the environment? The quick answer was "yes, no, or maybe." Pollution from noise and weapons use abated, fewer windows were broken by sonic booms, but plans for cleanup were minimal. Questions about the dangers of unexploded ordnance remained unanswered.

Tonopah Army Air Base

Seven miles west of Tonopah in Ralston Valley are the concrete skeletons of a large air base that flourished for five years during World War II. Even before the war, strategic planners for the U.S. Army selected the site, and in 1940 the War Department withdrew five thousand square miles of land from the public domain and began condemnation of private parcels to allow for bombing practice. The fast-paced construction produced runways, taxiways, about 140 buildings, a hospital, and a reservoir-pipeline system for the transmission of scarce water. The infrastructure was massive, and the construction work energized the economy of Tonopah as never before. At the peak of the operation, more than sixty-five hundred servicemen and workers were stationed at the base.

When World War II ended in 1945, abandonment of the facilities occurred even more rapidly than the construction. Building and assets were dispersed, but the scars of runways remained. Roads and giant hangars can still be seen from Highway 6. Later designated as the Tonopah Municipal Airport, it is a relic rather than the vital institution it once was. Decaying buildings and runways stand sixty years later as forlorn witnesses to a military venture now fading from memory.

Fallon Naval Air Station

The Fallon military base was a more resilient cousin of the Tonopah facility from the World War II era. It arose from the U.S. Navy's need for a secure place to train pilots who would eventually lift off from aircraft carriers to hit enemy targets at sea. The admirals chose a site near Fallon in the alkaline heart of the Carson Sink to instruct their pilots in the arts of aerial gunnery. Opening the Naval Auxiliary Landing Field in 1943, the military planners operated for three years and then deactivated the base as the peacetime agenda reappeared.

Then came the Korean War, and the Fallon Naval Air Station, unlike its counterpart at Tonopah, came online again. Because more of the infrastructure remained intact, the navy rejuvenated the old facilities for their inland training exercises. During the Vietnam War more than twenty-seven hundred personnel were stationed at Fallon.

A testimonial to the devastation wrought by the navy on the landscape can be found in *Bravo 20* by Richard Misrach and Myriam Weisang Misrach, a couple who fell in love with one of the most abused pieces of terrain in the way one might embrace a battered child. They wrote of the early years (1950–1980) of the military presence in Nevada: "For the next three decades they [the U.S. military establishment] would systematically weave their intricate network across the state—unhindered and for the most part welcome. The economy grew to depend on a steady influx of military dollars. Politicians regularly ran on pro-military platforms. Powerful bombers and jets became a familiar sight on the horizon, things of beauty and might which never failed to elicit awe, a touch of fear, and a thrill in those who looked on" (3).

Bravo 20 is located northeast of Fallon in the Carson Sink, between the Stillwater and Humboldt ranges. In the center of this 36-square-mile alkali flat a hill once existed, which rose about 250 feet above the basin floor. This became a favorite target for the navy bombardiers; over the years the hill became much lower. The surrounding landscape became a junkyard of enormous variety.

The Fallon Naval Air Station has three other bombing and gunnery ranges in addition to Bravo 20; they are located south of U.S. Highway 50 in the vicinity of the base. Yet another patch of earth is designated as an electronic-warfare training range. Several decades ago, about ten U.S. Navy photographs were made available to the Special Collections Department of the University of Nevada–Reno, providing snapshots of one of the targets. Labeled as B-16 "Billboard" Target Center Structures, the photos display a large screen that was repeatedly bombarded over a period of two months, July 5–September 7, 1960. During this time 1,302 aircraft made 6,944 "runs" on the target in thirty-seven days of operation.

This next fact may or may not be related to military operations: Fallon has experienced a frightening upsurge of childhood leukemia; seventeen diagnosed cases and three deaths were recorded between 1997 and 2005. Whether environmental changes caused this tragedy is unknown. The answer to this mystery is still being sought.

Hawthorne: Navy and Army Ammunition Storage

At the southern end of Walker Lake, in one of those wide, enticing valleys encircled by high desert mountains, sits Hawthorne. Here are the most endangered lake and one of the most tenacious towns in the Great Basin, as discussed in the previous chapter.

The ammunition depot that encircles the town has a longer history than the military bases at Las Vegas and Fallon. This site was chosen by the U.S. Navy in 1929 after a massive accidental explosion caused severe damage at a storage base in New Jersey. The remote location in Mineral County, Nevada, seemed appropriate then because of its isolation from large population centers. Hawthorne was an impoverished mining and railroad town of a few hundred people founded in 1881 that had never prospered. Nevada's political leaders and the local population welcomed the payrolls the navy could provide during the Great Depression.

The former Naval Ammunition Depot (NAD) extends over 240 square miles, including twenty-four hundred concrete bunkers or earth mounds, arranged in neat rows, where ammunition has been stored and reprocessed. The facilities are connected by more than 200 miles of railroads and more than 500 miles of paved roads. A 2,500-acre bomb-disposal site is operated about 25 miles from Hawthorne, and the army has reported that some areas have been contaminated by chemical agents and mustard gas. From the air, the depot has the look of a well-arranged cemetery.

It has become a sprawling mausoleum, but it was still functioning more than seventy-five years after its creation. When the navy no longer wanted NAD in the 1970s, the Pentagon transferred it to the army, which in 1980 transferred the duties to private contractors. In 2005 the Pentagon decided the depot was no longer needed for national defense and recommended abandonment. But the national commission responsible for military base closures rejected the proposal, and the depot survived for the time being.

The long-term ecological consequences of storing and exploding ammunition in the Walker Lake valley for decades have not been calculated. For more than seventy years, the ammunition depot was a mainstay of Hawthorne's economy, a sufficient local reason for its existence, but another open question for friends of the environment.

The M-X Episode

In the late 1970s, when the United States was locked in a deadly arms race with the Soviet Union, the Pentagon proposed a massive scheme for nuclear retaliation called m-x, or Missile Experimental. In theory, if the Communist USSR had ever launched an attack on America, the United States could have fired back with deadly force in an instant. On the advice of government public relations experts, the scheme was ironically called "Peacekeeper."

This grotesque scheme proposed to install two hundred missiles (each with ten nuclear warheads) in underground silos in Nevada and Utah. The missiles would have been capable of launching hundreds of warheads within a few minutes across the North Pole toward the Soviet Union, if any suspicious activity were detected halfway around the world. The missile locations were to be kept secret, and they would have been moved occasionally from one silo to another among forty-six hundred scattered locations. The government assured citizens that a potential enemy could never hope to hit all silos with a single attack. The fact that the United States already had a massive fleet of bombers and scores of nuclear submarines capable of incinerating the Soviet Union within a few hours did not satisfy the military strategists.

The proposal to deploy the m-x missiles in the "racetrack" mode gained the reluctant approval of President Jimmy Carter in June 1979. As the details unfolded over the next few months, the cost of construction—building the silos, the extensive network of roads and equipment, and related expenditures—was estimated at between thirty and sixty billion dollars. The implications for the economy of the entire Southwest were staggering. A main operation center was to be located about fifty miles north of Las Vegas, nearer to the city than most Nevada Test Site facilities.

Depending on one's point of view, here was an unprecedented economic opportunity for Nevada or a deadly challenge for the citizens of Las Vegas, upstate Nevada, southern California, and Utah.

Would M-X be good or bad for the regional economy and for the lifestyle westerners had assumed to be their birthright? Would it produce jobs (the recurring question), or would it make Nevadans on their desert frontier vulnerable to a "first strike" in the event of war? All the gambles that Nevadans had previously taken with military installations had been made on the assumption that they were far removed from any potential battlefront, out of the line of fire, remote from consequences. The M-X idea was different. For the next two years, public debate about M-X was the most controversial topic in the Far West. The U.S. Air Force sent spokesmen across Nevada and Utah to present a positive picture of the plan. Their professional admen tried to generate public support.

Federal laws required an environmental impact statement describing the possible consequences for the natural and human habitat. As more information became available, public reaction throughout the Southwest hardened against the idea. In the spring of 1980 the leaders of the Church of Jesus Christ of Latter-day Saints expressed their opposition to the plan. Even President Carter, who had originally let the racetrack silo idea go forward, was uneasy about it. He wrote in his diary on June 4, 1979, "I discussed my disappointment with the weekly memorandum on MX mobile basing. It was a nauseating prospect to confront, with the gross waste of money going into nuclear weapons of all kinds" (241).

In the 1980 election season, when Governor Ronald Reagan of California was challenging President Carter for the presidency, Reagan expressed opposition to the M-X racetrack scheme during his visits to the Far West. The vast majority of Nevadans had obviously made up their minds by this time; they did not like the proposal, and they did not trust the government's assurances. In an advisory referendum held in eight counties (but not in Clark County), forty-one thousand voters registered their opposition, whereas only nineteen thousand supported M-X. When in October 1981 President Reagan announced that the racetrack plan would be abandoned, most Nevadans were jubilant. Senator Paul Laxalt ultimately played a large part in scrapping the M-X plan. He was a close friend of newly elected President Reagan, and did not want Nevada to become a prime target for a Soviet military attack.

The two Las Vegas members of the Nevada congressional delegation, Senator Howard Cannon and Congressman James Santini, took opposite positions on the M-X question. Santini became an outspoken opponent of the missile plan. Cannon, on the other hand, long an advocate of air force interests in the Senate, gingerly supported it. He tried, unsuccessfully, to convince his constituents that the impact of the program could be beneficial, as the building of Hoover Dam had been in the 1930s. In 1982, when Cannon sought reelection to his fifth term in the Senate, Santini challenged him in the Democratic primary, and the two men engaged in a painful political conflict that damaged the reputations of both. Cannon survived this challenge in the primary election, but in the subsequent general election he lost his seat to a little-known Republican, Las Vegas businessman Chic Hecht. The controversy over the M-X proposal and Cannon's support of it were factors in this turn of events. That candidate Reagan endorsed the little-known Hecht helped tip the balance toward the challenger.

CHAPTER SIX

Faustian Laboratory of the Nuclear Age, 1950–1992

W hen the United States confronted its most challenging decisions in the twentieth century, it often looked to Nevada's
open spaces for solutions. During World War II and the Cold War,
southern Nevada became a preferred site for feverish military
spending. This desert state was exceptional in the variety of defense-
related enterprises tested on, under, and above its terrain. Nevada
enjoyed quick, profitable contracts and short-term benefits; it
learned belatedly that it had inherited another toxic legacy as well.

As Las Vegas became the hometown of Nellis Air Force Base,
the largest fighter-plane training facility in the nation, one million acres were withdrawn from the public domain in southern
Nevada to allow for bombing and gunnery practice. Then, in the
1950s, the federal government preempted a stretch of desert only
sixty-five miles from Las Vegas for the Nevada Test Site. This became the world's hottest, most deadly nuclear garbage dump. Even
more ominously, in the 1980s, because of the enormous stretches of seemingly barren terrain still available on the leeward side
of the southern Sierra Nevada, Yucca Mountain northwest of Las
Vegas became the preferred choice of the profit-making nuclear
industries as the place to bury the most dangerous residue of their

toxic refuse—thousands of tons of radioactive waste. (We will discuss this issue in the next chapter.)

Thus, the skies above Nevada, the surface area of tens of thousands of square miles, and the depths of its southern deserts were taken by the federal government for awesome missions that had little regard for the fragile environment. We must circle back again to earlier history to put this decision in perspective.

The Nevada Test Site

The opening of the nuclear age during World War II spawned not only atomic bombs like those dropped on Hiroshima and Nagasaki in 1945 but also a new era of scientific research on additional military uses of this form of energy. Inquiries about possible peaceful applications of atomic power followed. Over the next half century, as the U.S. government and private industry explored the potential uses and dangers of nuclear energy, they looked to southern Nevada for the same reasons that had existed in the 1940s when the air force located its tactical fighter base there—vast amounts of public land under federal control.

President Harry Truman announced the beginning of atomic testing in Nevada in 1951, two years after the Soviet Union exploded its first atomic bomb. For more than forty years, between January 1951 and October 1992, the center for American nuclear testing was a swath of terrain, carved from the Las Vegas–Tonopah Bombing and Gunnery Range and two desolate sites near Fallon in northwestern Nevada. The Nevada site initially contained 350 square miles; a series of expansions added another 1,000 square miles to the testing zone by 1968. The area was presumed to be a wasteland, chosen for its remoteness from population centers, for the favorable desert climatic conditions, and for its relatively secure geographical location, before a few sensitive Nevadans began to understand the implications of testing.

Las Vegas quickly felt the monetary benefits and enjoyed the new attention that followed the first tests in the atmosphere. Gladwin Hill of the *New York Times*, who visited the vicinity after five explosions had been detonated, made one of the first reports on the new experimentation. He considered the little city of some twenty-five thousand people, which he called "one of the most amiably raffish communities in the nation," an odd place for the conducting of such important scientific experiments. Yet Las Vegans took the new "industry" in stride and noticed an increase rather than a decline in visitors.

The Nevada Test Site became the world's most active center for the testing of nuclear devices. According to the *Bulletin of the Atomic Scientists*, at least 1,820 known nuclear tests were conducted throughout the world from the beginning of the atomic age in 1945 until the end of 1989. In this forty-five-year span, the United States acknowledged testing more than half the number detonated throughout the world and approximately 280 more than the Soviet Union. Of this number, U.S. government spokesmen affirmed, about 100 had been detonated on or above the earth's surface; 804 had been exploded in tunnels beneath the ground. Both the United States and the Soviet Union observed a moratorium on testing for nearly three years in 1958–1961, but when the experiments were resumed, the pace was more rapid than it had previously been. The peak year for testing was 1962.

Most aboveground tests were conducted during the early period, when the danger of radiation injury to humans and other organisms was not well understood by the public. The U.S. Army conducted troop maneuvers in the blast areas soon after test detonations occurred, assuring participants that such exercises were safe. The Pentagon routinely placed troops in trenches within two miles of the explosion site. Most early testing was designed to ascertain the hazards and efficiency of nuclear weapons for military use. Later research dealt with rocket propulsion and possible peaceful uses such as underground water diversions, development of fossil fuel reserves, and plans for canals, harbors, and highways. In the 1980s, belatedly, some research focused on the problems of the disposal of nuclear waste. The U.S. Atomic Energy Commission (AEC), the agency initially responsible for the research, repeatedly told the public that the testing was safe; it was seemingly sincere in its assurances. Programs such as Atoms for Peace and "Plowshare" reinforced the public relations efforts of the AEC in offering comfort to the wider audience.

In the mid-1970s Congress reorganized the administrative structure of the program, with the Department of Energy (DOE) replacing the AEC. This change had little impact locally. An entire industry and a new generation had grown up around the operation in southern Nevada, employing between eight and nine thousand people. With the end of the Cold War and the disappearance of the Soviet threat, the U.S. government began to scale back its long-term commitment to nuclear testing.

The Protest Movements

Although a few westerners had misgivings about nuclear testing in the early years, the general attitude of the local population reflected widespread support for the program. A few residents of southern Nevada and adjacent regions objected when they incurred property damage or when livestock owners noticed burn scars on their animals as a result of exposure to radiation. The eccentric industrialist Howard Hughes got harsh publicity for his strident opposition to the explosions, which he believed were occurring too near his cloistered residence on the Strip. The public, however, was generally silent or supported the testing. Few expressions of alarm were recorded locally about the possible hazards prior to the mid-1970s.

In 1975 a Nevada-based group calling itself Citizen Alert became the catalyst for a movement to inform the public about the scope and details of federal government activities in the state. This effort emerged in response to reports that the government might select a Nevada site for the burial of nuclear waste. Established by Katharine Hale and Susan Orr and financed largely by Nevada philanthropist Maya Miller, Citizen Alert mobilized the latent concerns into an effective siren call. The Shoshone Indians, who had long claimed about 60 percent of Nevada as their land (embodied in an 1863 treaty that had never been revoked), joined the movement. Bob Fulkerson, a young activist skilled in public outreach efforts, became the effective leader in publicizing the objections to the nuclear explosions and the possible nuclear dump site.

By 1980 regional and national perspectives on testing were clearly changing. A cluster of medical experts, working through an organization called Physicians for Social Responsibility, urged a test ban. As early as the 1970s, a coalition of religious organizations held peaceful protests against the activities at the Nevada Test Site regularly during the Christmas season and Lent in order to increase public awareness of the dangers of nuclear testing. Thousands of protesters gathered near the main gate of the test site during the Christian holy days for nonviolent civil disobedience. In a typical year the demonstrators received training in nonviolent behavior and in recommended conduct in the event of harassment and arrest. Inspired by the pacifist examples of Gandhi and Martin Luther King Jr., they made statements of conscience that often annoyed government agents, but they provoked no serious incidents. Records of these groups showed that during the 1980s more than thirty-six thousand participated, with eleven thousand arrested and arraigned, including several national religious leaders. Hundreds of protesters were transported by bus to the county seat in Tonopah, more than a hundred miles away, for the legal hearings. Most were quickly released and invited to find their own routes homeward. The government did not want to prosecute them, but only to cause inconvenience. Carl Sagan, the famous scientist, science-fiction writer, and Pulitzer Prize winner, was among the celebrities who brought attention to the protests.

In 1993 a powerful testimonial about the human costs of the testing appeared in a book published by New York photographer and writer Carole Gallagher. For more than a decade, Gallagher took photographs and recorded interviews with people who had worked at the test site and residents of Utah who had lived down-wind from it between 1951 and 1963, when tests were conduct-ed in the atmosphere. The result is a devastating indictment of government agencies and the policies that subjected thousands of westerners to large doses of atomic radiation while assuring them that the tests were safe. Her book documents a program of repeated deceptions and evasions that led to the deaths and illnesses of hun-dreds of individuals living at or near the test site. Keith Schneider sets the tone for the volume in the foreword: "The Soviet Union was condemned by the United States for keeping the Chernobyl disaster secret for three days and preventing Ukrainians and Europeans from taking measures to protect themselves from the radiation. In contrast, the leaders of the American nuclear weap-ons industry waged a secret medical and scientific struggle for 30 years to cover up the contamination of vast areas of North America from atomic blasts at the Nevada Test Site" (xv).

Gallagher's book was only one item in a sequence of testimoni-als against the testing policy that had been in effect for more than forty years. The problem can be brought into focus and personal-ized by the case of Keith Prescott of Salt Lake City, who had sloshed radioactive muck from the tunnels at the test site in the 1960s. Without realizing he was doing so, he had placed his life on the line for a miner's wages and in the interest of national defense. Later recurring symptoms—nausea, headaches, and pain—forced him to retire. He sued the government in 1979 and lived long enough to sustain his suit for fourteen years. An essential question before federal judge Philip Pro was whether a connection could be made between Prescott's cancer and the radiation exposure he experi-enced at the test site during his employment there.

Another eloquent case against nuclear testing and the gov-ernment's attitude toward it appears in Rebecca Solnit's *Savage Dreams*, which combines an environmental activist's strategy with insights from the world of classical painting and a profound de-scription of the opening of the nuclear age. She regards herself and her companions as Acadians engaged in a mortal and moral struggle with the Utopians who are bent on redesigning the world. As one who has explored the various desert regions with empathy and repeatedly tried to breach the security barriers around the test site, she offers personal testimonials that are lyrical in tone and tough-minded in their logic. In her view the American government, in its nuclear testing program, was waging a war against its people and "had been rehearsing the end of the world out here, over and over again" (5).

The Test Ban Moratorium of the 1990s

Partly in response to protests but mainly because of the 1991 collapse of the Soviet Union, Congress in October 1992 passed the Nuclear Test Moratorium Act, suspending experiments for nine months and sharply limiting the number of tests that could be undertaken after that time. When the deadline for the suspension passed in July 1993, President Clinton extended the moratorium, indicating that the United States would not restart testing in the foreseeable future unless foreign countries resumed disturbing levels of research and development in the nuclear field. He renewed the suspension again in 1995, making his decision against the advice of the Department of Defense and others in the military establishment but in concert with growing public sentiment against further testing. More than a hundred members of the House of Representatives and at least thirty-six senators were on record against the resumption of testing. President Clinton's action extending the testing moratorium put the future of the test site on hold, although it was assumed that important work on development or disposal of atomic weaponry would continue. The Department of Energy projected that the Nevada Test Site workforce would be reduced significantly. The continuing legacy of pollution was only marginally addressed in the official budgets of the U.S. government.

Even as the future of the Nevada Test Site was under review, archaeologists from the University of Nevada's Desert Research

Institute (DRI) recommended that parts of the locale be considered for listing on the National Register of Historic Places. The debris from scores of blasts that occurred above the earth's surface at Frenchman Flat left significant evidence of the destructive power of the bombs.

In 2005 the University of Nevada, Las Vegas expanded an oral history program to interview dozens of test site scientists, workers, and protesters about the events of the previous decades of nuclear testing. A group of former test site employees organized to establish the Nevada Test Site Museum near the university to collect data, photos, and memorabilia from the years of active testing. It has become an affiliate of the Smithsonian Institution of Washington, D.C.

CHAPTER SEVEN

Nuclear Waste

As the debate about the m-x racetrack scheme receded from the horizon in Nevada, an even more challenging threat loomed. It involved the question of how the nation would dispose of its growing stockpile of deadly nuclear garbage, which had been accumulating for more than thirty years.

Throughout the previous three decades, the U.S. government and the private nuclear industry had been building atomic power—generating reactors in many parts of the country. At first, it seemed likely that the new technology would meet America's need for cheap energy for decades. But there was a downside. As the nuclear power plants went into operation and expanded, they created thousands of tons of high-level nuclear waste that will be hazardous for centuries—perhaps for ten millennia. Neither the government nor the power-generating companies had identified a safe way to dispose of this refuse. What if our family garbage bins were full of putrid matter and no garbage trucks were available?

In 1954 Congress passed the Atomic Energy Act, a crucial piece of legislation in encouraging the expansion of the industry. It promoted a program for subsidizing uranium mining and assisting the private development of nuclear plants. The Atomic Energy

Commission operated as both the promoter and the regulator of the burgeoning industry. Yet the toxic detritus piled up.

For the next quarter century, as the nuclear power industry expanded, there was little public opposition to the growing number of atomic reactors, because they seemed to produce additional energy at lower cost with less air pollution than oil or coal. Most of the public was either indifferent or regarded it as a good way to meet growing energy needs in areas that lacked cheap hydroelectrical power and had problems of air pollution, especially the Northeast and Midwest. Neither the government nor the utilities industry directly addressed the problem of waste disposal. State and local governments were given no voice in making nuclear energy policy, but gradually they became centers of opposition as the question of waste disposal became more evident.

By the end of the 1960s, nuclear waste was accumulating at more than sixty sites where power plants operated and at many federal facilities where weapons had been produced. In 1975 the Nevada legislature, in a joint resolution approved by a majority in both houses, invited the federal government to consider establishing a nuclear depository in Nevada. At the end of the 1970s—a decade when environmental concerns were more acute—the private nuclear power industry became sufficiently worried about its growing inventory of hazardous waste to seek congressional help. Some waste was stored in liquid form in unstable metal barrels, some in dangerous spent-fuel rods. In 1979 a reactor accident occurred at Three-Mile Island, Pennsylvania. At about the same time, a disturbing film titled *China Syndrome* reached the movie theaters. An antinuclear march brought thousands of citizens to the streets of the nation's capital. Opposition to building new reactors and to opening those under construction grew intense across the nation from Diablo Canyon, California, to Seabrook, New Hampshire. Scores of nuclear power plants under construction or on the planning boards were abandoned. The nationwide protest against the proliferation of nuclear plants caught the utilities industry and the government by surprise.

For many years Las Vegas, with its ample sources of electrical energy from the Colorado River dams and other local facilities, seemed exempt from this problem. No nuclear power–generating plants operated in the vicinity, but with the passage of the next major piece of nuclear energy legislation, southern Nevada was once again near a potential ground zero, and another Faustian bargain was offered.

The Nuclear Waste Policy Act of 1982

Congress passed the Nuclear Waste Policy Act (NWPA) of 1982 during the rush to adjourn three days before Christmas. It was a long, complicated bill, subject to many bargains and compromises in the final days of the congressional session. During the deliberations that preceded passage, several possible sites were considered for a permanent underground depository to hold the highly dangerous residue that would be radioactive for as long as ten thousand years. Locations in Utah, Washington, Texas, Louisiana, and Mississippi had been under consideration, as well as Yucca Mountain in Nevada. This legislation focused on only two or three possible sites, chosen for political rather than scientific reasons. The U.S. Geological Survey, the government agency responsible for evaluating the earth beneath us, recommended that more systematic scientific research be undertaken before a short list was finalized.

The Department of Energy was spending $270 million annually by 1982, much of it to try to find a repository, but it was apparent early in the process that more attention went to Yucca Mountain than to the other possibilities. Public confidence in the DOE declined in the 1980s as the agency came under increasing criticism from other government bureaus, from congressmen, and repeatedly from Nevada's political leaders. Governor Richard Bryan (1983–1989) was especially vociferous in his opposition to the federal government's preference for the Yucca Mountain site.

In 1987 controversy escalated both within and outside Nevada when Congress passed an amendment to the NWPA that eliminated all sites except Yucca Mountain from further consideration. This decision was not based on scientific evidence but made for political reasons; the nuclear power industry argued that the evaluation of three sites was too expensive. The new law chose Yucca Mountain by default, subject to further scientific investigation, which proceeded more slowly than expected. The 1987 amendment came to be known locally as the "Screw Nevada Bill." Yucca Mountain became the only choice because the DOE and atomic energy contractors had made such extensive investment there; they argued it was not economical to consider other possibilities.

Because the Nevada governmental agencies were initially ill-prepared to meet the challenge presented by the NWPA and the possibility of a dangerous nuclear repository being established in the state, the 1985 legislature established the Agency for Nuclear Projects (ANP), supplemented by the Commission on Nuclear Projects, to advise the governor and legislature. The ANP, under the direction of Robert Loux, was for the next twenty years the key department in gathering and distributing information about the ongoing activities of the DOE and the nuclear power industry. It also enabled Nevada to make official and systematic responses to changing conditions.

One provision of the NWPA provided that any state in which a depository was to be located had the right to refuse to accept the facility unless its objections were overridden by both houses of Congress. Nevada's legislature accepted the challenge in the short run, but in its next session after Congress passed the 1987 amendment, both the Nevada Senate and the Nevada Assembly overwhelmingly passed resolutions objecting to the designation of Yucca Mountain and refusing to accept the depository. There was widespread apprehension for the next several years that Congress would override Nevada's objections, but this happened only in 2002. Complex litigation developed between the DOE and Nevada state agencies because Nevada declined to grant permits for some DOE proposals, including use of underground water, until pertinent issues were resolved by federal courts. Federalism, in the conservative meaning of that term, was operating to retard a dangerous national government juggernaut.

Meanwhile, other ominous facts became evident. The NWPA had presumably set a maximum limit of seventy-seven thousand tons (or seventy thousand metric tons) of hazardous material that might be stored at Yucca Mountain. Yet by 1993 it was evident that the nation already needed storage space for substantially more than one hundred thousand metric tons to handle the waste coming from nuclear power plants and Department of Defense facilities. The original intent of the 1982 legislation had been to provide the depository only for refuse from the nuclear power industry, with a provision that the president could decide whether to locate high-level nuclear waste from defense-related operations in the same place.

Public skepticism about the plan grew more intense as time passed. In 1991 the American Nuclear Energy Council, an organization sponsored by the profit-seeking nuclear power–producing companies, decided to launch a three-year, $8.7 million public relations campaign to persuade Nevada residents that the idea of a nuclear waste depository at Yucca Mountain was sound. The advertisements, mostly on television, stressed the safety of proposed storage and generous economic benefits that would flow from the depository. Early in the campaign, it became evident that the advertising had backfired. A plan to lobby state legislators, to woo the Nevada Resort Association, and gradually to outmaneuver state politicians and the media became known before it could gain headway. In short order the state government, well-organized nonprofit groups, and private agencies mounted their own countercampaigns. Local opposition became more—not less—intense as a result of the advertising.

Recurring earthquakes in southern California and Nevada added to the uneasiness that residents felt about the repository proposal. In June 1992 a 5.6-magnitude seismic event occurred at Little Skull Mountain, about twelve miles from Yucca Mountain, on a previously unidentified fault; notable changes in groundwater levels occurred as a result. This earthquake did a million dollars in damage to the DOE facilities at Yucca Mountain.

The controversy between the DOE and its critics grew as additional government agencies became critical of the procedures that the DOE used in conducting its examination of the site. A team of geologists sponsored by the National Academy of Sciences reported early in 1993 that it found DOE studies of the hydrological features of the area to be inadequate. The General Accounting Office, the congressional research agency that scrutinizes the executive branch departments, reported in May 1993 that the DOE had spent its money inefficiently and that the process of site selection would require much more time than originally anticipated. The ABC television network on July 19, 1993, discussed allegations that the DOE, which initially planned to spend $70 million studying the Yucca Mountain site, now expected to spend more than $6 billion on its research there.

Nevada citizens were vociferous in objecting to the unique designation of Yucca Mountain site for consideration. Between 1982 and 2007 each Nevada governor—Robert List, Richard Bryan, Bob Miller, and Kenny Guinn—and all of Nevada's congressional delegation opposed the effort to force the depository on Nevada. In 1993 a small group of state senators proposed to the state legislature that their Committee on High Level Nuclear Waste be allowed to begin tentative negotiations with the DOE to learn more about the benefits that would come to the state in the event a repository were placed in Nevada. The bill was soundly defeated in the senate on one of the last days of the session.

One obvious reason Nevada was a favored target for the unwanted depository was its long-standing unsavory reputation. In the 1990s, a Las Vegas mayor, Jan Lafferty Jones, quipped that some people believed Las Vegas deserved the nuclear waste dump, because if such a facility was necessary, it should be located near a city where everyone lives in casinos and nobody goes to school.

The DOE initially set 1997 as the target date for possible opening of the Yucca Mountain repository, but by all standards its work of site characterization lagged far behind schedule. No consensus existed among scientists early in the twenty-first century about whether the location was sufficiently safe from earthquakes or remote enough from deep aquifers of water to render it safe before the year 12000.

Nevada and the nation were engaged in the largest gamble yet undertaken by humankind as the decision makers lurched and stumbled toward establishing a nuclear waste site at Yucca Mountain. President Bill Clinton's secretary of energy, Hazel O'Leary, who had led a movement to uncover the results of nuclear testing of the 1950s and 1960s, would not rule out the possibility that Yucca Mountain might be used as a "temporary" storage site for unwanted nuclear fuel debris. During the two terms of President Clinton, the final decision on Yucca Mountain was deferred.

Managing Other Toxic DOE Sites

The U.S. government regularly reports on its management of toxic waste stored in various parts of the country. It routinely uses gentle terms, cushioned by bland technical prose meant to soothe as it informs. It remains for the journalists and historians to provide the larger context.

In January 2001 the Department of Energy published its analysis of four sites in Nevada over which it had "long-term stewardship" responsibility. Three are smaller than the Nevada Test Site but also potentially highly toxic. They are the Tonopah Test Range; the Central Nevada Test Area, 60 miles northeast of Tonopah; and the so-called Project Shoal, southeast of Fallon. The Nevada Test Site sprawls over 1,375 square miles just an hour's drive northwest of Las Vegas and contains some of the most dangerous nuclear residue on earth.

The Tonopah Test Range, a dormant relic, is a small component of America's vast military-industrial complex. Consisting of 624 square miles, it was withdrawn from the public domain in the 1940s by the U.S. Air Force and has been used since 1956 for developing weapons delivery systems and electronic training assignments.

The Central Nevada Test Area is a relatively small (2,560-acre) site in northeastern Nye County, where a single nuclear device was exploded underground in 1968. This test was designed to study the behavior of seismic waves and to determine whether that location was suitable for larger experiments; the evidence was negative, and northern Nye County was spared the fate of the landscape farther south. In the late 1990s the DOE worked at surface decontamination in anticipation of turning the site over to the Department of Interior and Department of Agriculture. One objective was to try to learn how groundwater had been affected. The government stewards had one major caveat about the future of the Central Nevada Site, though: "[The] DOE does not plan to remediate the subsurface contamination because of the lack of feasible technologies for removing subsurface contamination from the site" (U.S. Department of Energy, Office of Environmental Management, 3). In other words, the so-called stewards did not know what to do with the toxic legacy of a blast conducted more than thirty years earlier only 3,200 feet underground and far beyond the Nevada Test Site. The annual cost of the stewardship from 2000 through 2006 was estimated to be $37,000—a piddling budget for a toxic site, even if it survives the perennial budget cuts.

Project Shoal is a 2,560-acre site located about thirty miles southeast of Fallon, near U.S. Highway 50. The Atomic Energy Commission detonated one 12-kiliton device there at a depth of about 1,200 feet in 1963 to test the feasibility of an underground experiment in granite rock and to learn more about the possibility of detecting such tests. The DOE, which assumed responsibility from the AEC for the testing, completed its remediation efforts on the surface in 1998 and turned its monitoring responsibilities over to the Department of Defense. The DOE retains responsibility for checking on subsurface contamination (U.S. Department of Energy, Office of Environmental Management, 49).

By far, though, the most deadly refuse pile in the United States is the Nevada Test Site, where nuclear weapons have been tested for a half century. It includes 1.27 million acres of land (an area about the size of Rhode Island), holding some of the most radioactive garbage on the planet. Surrounded on three sides by Nellis Air Force Base, the site was originally presumed to have a sufficient buffer to ensure secrecy and to shield the neighboring world from the radiation generated by the nuclear blasts. This lateral cushion of space proved deficient, however, because radiation from the tests lofted upward to join the prevailing westerly winds. They spread not only across nearby Nevada and Utah counties but also above the heartland of middle America for thousands of miles, dropping their lethal cargo willy-nilly. Unfortunately, government agencies did not detect this fact until many years later.

In February 2002 reports became available indicating a rise in deaths from thyroid cancer, presumably related to the nuclear testing. In the approximately one hundred tests conducted on or aboveground between 1951 and 1963, much of the radiation blew over Utah, Colorado, Wyoming, Nebraska, Iowa, Missouri, and Illinois. Although the Soviet Union was also conducting tests at the same time, the Nevada experiments were presumed to be partly responsible for increases in the incidence of thyroid cancer within the United States. In 1986 Congress belatedly passed the Radiation Victims' Compensation Act, which provided as much as $50,000 per person to individuals who could show their illnesses had resulted from the fallout.

Considering the billions invested by the U.S. government in nuclear testing and weapons development, the amount anticipated for stewardship at the Nevada Test Site was minuscule—only $1.54 million per year from 2001 through 2006. The large casinos on the Las Vegas Strip process that amount of money in a few hours of gambling frolic.

Decision Time: The Year 2002 and George W. Bush

Soon after the beginning of the new century and the inauguration of President George W. Bush, the program changed. For two decades the DOE had proceeded with its engineering work at Yucca Mountain while Nevada and its environmental allies mustered and called attention to scientific and environmental questions. The standoff reached a decisive point early in 2002 when Secretary of Energy Spencer Abraham recommended to President Bush that Yucca Mountain be selected as the site for the permanent storage of nuclear waste. The president forwarded this suggestion to Congress, as provided for in the 1982 act. Again, the justification was political rather than scientific.

Secretary Abraham (formerly a U.S. senator from Michigan) had been a special friend of the nuclear power industry while he was in Congress. He had received generous contributions from these companies during his political campaigns. Soon after September 11, 2001, when suicidal terrorists flew airliners into the World Trade Center and the Pentagon, Abraham cited the threat of future attacks as a rationale for concentrating the hazardous material in Nevada, and President Bush quickly endorsed the plan. This finalized the executive branch decision to approve the Yucca Mountain depository.

Nevada's governor and congressional delegation did their best to block the decision in Congress, but they failed because there was not enough support for Nevada's position among eastern members of the House and Senate. The nuclear power industry had given more than $30 million to favorite candidates during the previous decade. Although outgunned, Nevada's political leaders did not flinch. The 2003 legislature faced severe financial problems, but it funded the continuation of the lawsuits pending in the courts, and this tenacity bore fruit. Governor Kenny Guinn and Senator Harry Reid continued to be outspoken critics of the dump-site plans throughout the controversy.

A victory for Nevada and the environmentalists came in July 2004, when a federal appeals court in the District of Columbia ruled that the existing federal government standards for ensuring safety from radiation contamination were inadequate. The court asserted that a ten thousand–year holding period for the contaminated waste might not be enough. More evidence was needed. The appeals court rejected one of Nevada's less credible legal claims: that the U.S. Constitution protected a state from the necessity of accepting a project it did not want. Thus, the old states' rights doctrine that Nevada's attorneys had often asserted in the past failed once again. It was a feeble line of defense, with little relevance to the main case. The decision of the appeals court in Washington was based on firmer legal ground—that the environmental standards used by the federal government were inadequate. It was a powerful victory for environmentalists who seek to protect the fragile ecology of the basin and range province from the ultimate pollutants imposed by runaway politics. This ruling delayed the date for the opening of the depository beyond 2010.

By 2008 the federal government had spent more than $9 billion trying to develop and promote the idea of safe disposal. The project was still on hold, but the DOE issued its *Final Supplemental Environmental Impact Statement* (*SEIS*) in June, offering updated assessments about building and maintaining the repository. Divided into two parts, the *SEIS* included the standard reassurances about the safety and feasibility of the proposal. It anticipated shipments of nuclear waste from seventy-two commercial sites and four DOE locations across the country. The *Final SEIS* speculated on environmental impact for ten thousand—or perhaps a million—years. The statement assumed a construction period of five years, an analytical period of one hundred years, and closure of the site after another ten-year period. Another assumption is that the DOE's construction operations would begin in 2017 and end about ten years later.

A second part anticipated a new railroad from Caliente to Yucca Mountain. It would move like a snake through the mountains and valleys of central Nevada. It must be north of the Nevada Test Site and reach Goldfield. Then it would shift to the southeast to the depository, covering a distance of about 330 miles. The cost estimates ranged from $2.5 to $3 billion.

As the years passed, Nevadans became increasingly skeptical of the assurances of the federal government and the nuclear power industry. This distrust was magnified by persistent reports of secret activities at Groom Mountain, located in the vast arid region between Las Vegas, Tonopah, and Alamo. Secret activities were reportedly conducted there for unknown purposes. Rumors persisted that human lives had been lost, which the government denied. This was another instance in which the environmental impact was unknown and perhaps unknowable.

Behind these considerations was an eerie feeling that decisions had been made that went much beyond the question of the short-term impact on southern Nevada and its near neighbors. To contemplate the problems that might be encountered by future generations over a span of twelve thousand years as a result of contemporary political pressures seemed beyond the intellectual capabilities of those engaged in the enterprise. Is it conceivable that the current generation, at its present level of technological sophistication, can decide how to store the waste safely, marking the site with warnings that can be read ten or twelve thousand years from now, and guarding against future seismic and other events that could render the nuclear risks fatal for civilization? The decision to bury such waste may be irrevocable—the most daring Faustian bargain ever taken in human experience. So southern Nevada surges onward, laboratory to Nevada, the nation, and the world. The consequences of the bargain are unknown.

CHAPTER EIGHT

Referees and Reformers

The activities of those who are altering Nevada's rugged but fragile landscape with weaponry, giant shovels, trucks, and bulldozers are superficially known to that part of the public who are listening and watching. Their noise resembles the sound of artillery shells lobbed onto a nearby battlefield, within earshot but far enough away to seem not immediately threatening. We are occasionally warned by the news media about these events, but our individual responses are mixed. Are we now being awakened from our snooze?

The voices of those who are trying to identify and mitigate environmental damage are less audible. They try to be the watchmen of this enterprise, hoping to retard and reverse the continuing degradation of the lands and waters.

The Federal Agencies

"The Great Basin is in trouble.... A large part of the Great Basin lies on the brink of ecological collapse." This ominous warning came at the dawn of the new millennium in a publication of the Bureau of Land Management dated April 2000. It was published soon after the disastrous rangeland fires of 1999, but it has broader applications.

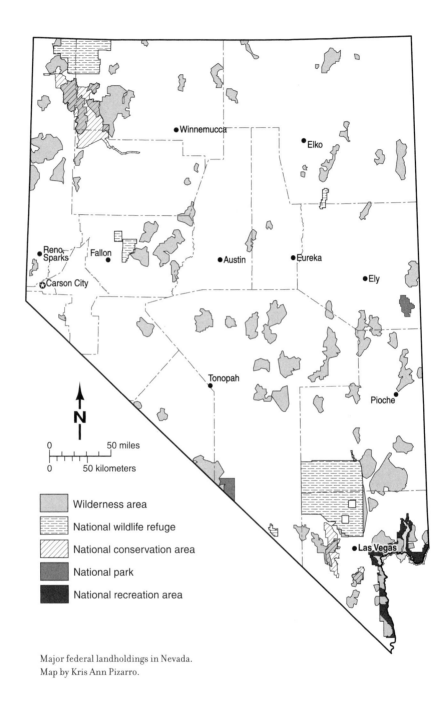

Major federal landholdings in Nevada.
Map by Kris Ann Pizarro.

Because the federal government owns most of the land in Nevada, its agencies have most of the responsibility for protecting the environment in the 95 percent of Nevada beyond the cities and towns. Of the approximately 70.2 million acres within the borders, civilian federal agencies manage 58.37 million acres, or about 83 percent—a higher proportion than in any other state. The pioneer era when the U.S. government was trying to dispose of its land quickly and cheaply is long past, although echoes of that policy are still heard in the public discourse. During the late twentieth century, official federal policy evolved into a philosophy of "steward-ship," which assumed that most public land resources should be retained and protected for long-term multiple uses. This concept has long been controversial in rural Nevada, and since 2000 it has been challenged by some attitudes within the executive branch of the federal government itself.

The Bureau of Land Management

One of the most vital U.S. government agencies operating in Nevada is the Bureau of Land Management; it is also one of the most controversial. The BLM, a division of the Department of Interior, has responsibility for managing most of the government-owned land—nearly 48 million acres, or about two-thirds of the state's landscape. The military, the Forest Service, the Department of Energy, Indian tribes, and other agencies also administer substantial tracts, but none arouses the level of debate that the BLM has known over the past four decades.

The BLM, a descendent of the Public Land Office that was eager to dispose of the public lands in the nineteenth century, has a totally different mission from its predecessor. Its new roles and responsibilities evolved in the last half of the twentieth century. Established by Congress in 1946, its current mission (as of 2009) is to improve and repair the public lands that have been abused and to make them available for many public uses.

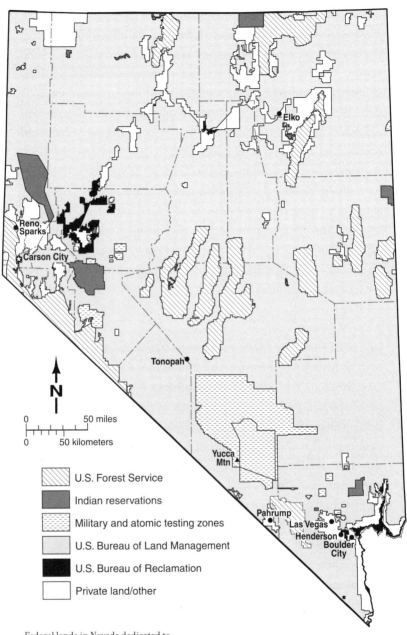

Federal lands in Nevada dedicated to
conservation and recreation. Map by
Kris Ann Pizarro.

The scope of BLM responsibility is huge. It not only monitors the activities of mining companies and livestock owners who graze animals on the public domain but also provides licenses to those who want to drill for oil and gas or generate geothermal power. It seeks to protect twenty-five designated wilderness areas and hundreds of historical sites in Nevada, encourage outdoor recreational activities, manage large herds of wild horses and burros, and fight cheatgrass and other invasive weeds. A related responsibility is to reduce the threat of wildfires to lives and the landscape. The BLM has launched the Great Basin Restoration Initiative to repair the areas blackened by the intense blazes of the past decade. Its budget is meager, and declining in view of the challenges it faces. And in the early twenty-first century, it operates within a federal administration unsympathetic to its mandate. The broad range of responsibilities assigned to the BLM has been controversial. Like a sheriff assigned to bring order to an unruly frontier town (or in this case a sprawling frontier state), the assignment is especially delicate in Nevada. BLM agents are mandated to reduce overgrazing, mitigate exploitation of resources by the mining industry, and protect wilderness and wild horses. The BLM workers on the ground in Nevada must be sometimes partners to the environmentalists, but they are regarded as intruders by those who are hostile to the federal government.

In recent years the BLM has been authorized to sell limited federal holdings in Las Vegas Valley to accommodate the urban population expansion. In exchange, the federal government has gained some sensitive forestlands in the northern Sierra Nevada. This land-swapping business seems, from the layman's perspective, to be a good deal for all parties. But again, a few environmentalists assert that it does not give proper regard to the delicate lands in Clark County.

The U.S. Forest Service

More than six million acres of Nevada's mountainous terrain are the responsibility of the U.S. Forest Service, which had its one hundredth birthday in 2005. It is about fifty years older than its distant cousin, the BLM; its venue is generally in the high country rather than in the gray valley rangelands. Therefore, it has been more readily accepted by most Nevadans than the BLM.

The U.S. Forest Service in Nevada manages the largest segment of forested land in the lower forty-eight states; only Alaska has more acreage in this category. These regions are administered within the Department of Agriculture (not Interior); in Nevada its political turf is usually on the fringes of the contentious environmental battles.

Like the BLM, the Forest Service is committed to multiple uses of the public lands under its control. Both agencies were making extraordinary efforts in 2006 and beyond to prevent another season of destructive wildfires after a wet winter. The spread of cheatgrass and other flammable underbrush in the hot, dry summers made this task more daunting than in the past.

As the years pass, its responsibility grows; the Carson Ranger District is one example. A map of Forest Service lands adjacent to Lake Tahoe in 1960 shows a few small patches of green around the lake and along the Nevada-California border within its jurisdiction. A comparable map for 2000 has many more large green blocks, representing mountain and foothill areas that have been purchased, traded, or given to the Forest Service for restoration. The forestlands of the eastern Sierra Nevada were being better cared for at the beginning of the twenty-first century than ever before. But destructive forest fires were also more common.

BLM and Forest Service personnel on the ground, who are both devoted citizens and public servants, face repeated challenges from intentional vandals, careless polluters, and unintentional arsonists. Forest Service and BLM signs are frequently defaced and damaged. Most fires in brushland and forests are caused by human activity. An expanding problem for forest rangers and the general public is the growing number of off-road vehicles, whose users are often careless with their matches and exhaust vapors.

Another challenge is the urban sprawl in the Reno area; as of 2006, twenty thousand new homes were being planned west of Reno in the Truckee Canyon region and along the Sierra Nevada foothills. The city of Reno now abuts the national forests to its west and approaches a region designated as wilderness.

Las Vegas did not have exactly the same problem because its city limits were still distant from the Mount Charleston segment of Forest Service lands. But along the fringes of the valley, land trades with the federal government had been supplemented by land auctions managed by the BLM. This has put much more of southern Nevada's terrain in the possession of developers. The Southern Nevada Public Land Management Act of 1998 expanded BLM responsibility in releasing land for development. This arrangement set off alarm bells for environmentalists, including the ever watchful Sierra Club.

The urban expansion around Las Vegas and Henderson, Reno and Carson, and Minden and Gardnerville may be consuming more land than the controversial mining activities in the high desert of the Great Basin. Who is to say which is more serious? Considering Nevada's recent evolution, what does the future hold? This manuscript seeks to ask the questions, but it cannot provide many answers.

The Environmental Protection Agency

A more recent addition to the federal ecological team is the Environmental Protection Agency, established in 1970. Environmental activism had reached a fever pitch in the United States in the late 1960s. When Congress overwhelmingly passed the National Environmental Policy Act (NEPA) late in 1969, President Richard M. Nixon reluctantly signed it into law in January 1970. It changed the ecolegal landscape in the nation and Nevada for a decade.

Throughout the 1970s, NEPA empowered private citizens to challenge polluters as never before. It mandated environmental impact statements when federal projects threatened the local ecological balance. On the basis of this law, Nevadans were able to challenge the m-x proposal. As discussed in chapter 5, that ill-conceived boondoggle died quietly, after a vocal and sustained public protest and sufficient scientific data pronounced it uneconomical and unworkable.

The EPA moved ahead through the 1970s, implementing safeguards at known toxic sites across America, including the notorious Love Canal pollution in New York. The environmental gains made by NEPA in the 1970s stalled in the 1980s after Ronald Reagan became president. A leading environmental historian based at the University of Nevada, Las Vegas wrote, "Under Reagan, the EPA suffered. During the first year of the new administration, the agency lacked an administrator. A sharp decline in new enforcement cases, a resulting loss of credibility for the agency, and dwindling morale among career employees marked the first two years under Reagan. A procession of weak and controversial leaders hamstrung the EPA throughout the mid-eighties as Americans felt their faith in the agency betrayed" (Rothman, *Saving the Planet* 196). The agency was further weakened after 2000 during the presidency of George W. Bush.

Back to the Land: Great Basin National Park

Let us step back for a moment from the larger problem of environmental challenges and reflect on one isolated success story. The crown jewel of Nevada's earliest landscape is the Great Basin National Park in White Pine County. This 77,180-acre region finally became a part of the national park system in 1986, following protracted resistance by local livestock and mining interests and a reactionary Nevada congressman.

The enclave includes the most delicate part of the rugged Snake Range, including 13,063-foot Wheeler Peak and the exotic Lehman Caves. It is Nevada's only national park, smaller than it might have been if there had been less resistance from the small number of traditional grazing users and miners. It required several years to phase out livestock grazing within the park, but in the past two decades it has enjoyed substantially more protection from abuse than in the previous hundred years.

Scientific journals repeatedly testify that our national parks are in danger. A century after the heroic work of John Muir and Theodore Roosevelt, many of the nation's most treasured natural sites are threatened; from the Smoky Mountains of Tennessee to the Big Bend of Texas and Death Valley in California and Nevada, air pollution from distant sources or local overuse is growing. Great Basin Natural Park, relatively remote from tourism and pollution, is less endangered than most at the moment.

Nevada's State Watchdogs
The Nevada State Environmental Commission

In 1971, when the American people were becoming more acutely aware of the environmental challenges facing the nation, Nevada's governor, Mike O'Callaghan, created an environmental task force by executive order. Newly elected with the wind of popular support in his sails, this dynamic chief executive, who loved the land, decided Nevada had to address its problems of pollution. In that same year, the state legislature established the predecessor to the Nevada State Environmental Commission (NSEC). As usual in such matters, the prompting for the legislation came from Washington. Congress passed and President Nixon signed in 1970 a law mandating the states to establish their own agencies to retard the growing air pollution.

Nevada's legislature, prodded by the governor and the federal government, established a commission on the environment. In its early years the leadership of the new commission came mainly from former rural legislators whose intention was to protect local industries (primarily mining and grazing) from being affected by the new federal regulations. Former state senator John Fransway spoke for most fellow commissioners when he said his mission was to keep "the feds" out of Nevada. A combination of meager budgets, a skeleton staff, and internal squabbling made the NSEC relatively ineffective until the 1990s.

Over the years, the commission adopted some stringent rules regarding air pollution affecting cities. It was perceived to have extensive authority under state statutes to reduce other environmental threats. The controversies around its operation often related to its membership, which mainly came from the industries or interests being "regulated." Representatives of the mining, agricultural, and construction businesses and at least one rural spokesman were guaranteed places on the commission by law. Its eleven members meet five or six times a year. Its staff support for implementing its mandate comes from the NDEP.

Environmental groups attempted during the 2003 and 2005 sessions of the legislature to add a provision to the law that would require the appointment of an environmentalist to the NSEC, but their efforts failed. The NSEC oversees the work of the Nevada Division of Environmental Protection.

The Nevada Division of Environmental Protection

The partner agency within state government that has on-the-ground responsibility for keeping an eye on threats to the ecosystem is the Nevada Division of Environmental Protection. It has a relatively small staff (about 240 persons) and a modest budget for the task assigned; its mandate is much broader than its resources.

The NDEP is a young agency within the state government, originating in the 1970s as an offspring of the state's Department of Health. Over the years it was assigned a wide range of responsibilities for monitoring pollution and hazards to the state's environment. It operates through nine units responsible for administration and the Bureaus of Air Quality Planning, Air Pollution Control, Water Pollution Control, Water Quality Planning, Mining Regulation and Reclamation, Corrective Actions, Waste Management, and Federal Facilities.

Worry about air pollution, especially in the urban areas, has been a concern of the division from its early days. Applying federal standards, the NDEP decided in the 1990s that the air was relatively clean over most of rural Nevada, but "serious" pollution from carbon monoxide and dust existed in Las Vegas Valley. Air-quality watchdogs in the valley face a serious challenge. With a rapidly growing population, scores of construction projects in the nearby desert, a burgeoning tourist business, and the exponential increase in auto traffic, this basin has air pollution problems greater than most large cities. The Truckee Meadows area (Reno and Sparks) and the Nevada side of the Lake Tahoe Basin were found to have "moderate" nonattainment of the national health standards. Thus, although most of rural Nevada has "clean" air, the regions where 80 percent of its citizens live do not. Auto emissions, wood burning, and industrial exhausts account for much of the problem. Pollutants in the urban areas include sulfur dioxide, carbon monoxide, nitrogen dioxide, ozone, particulate matter (dust), and lead. (Lead has been removed from gasoline in recent years, so presumably this risk has been reduced.) The NDEP reports that risks from air pollution diminished during the 1990s; the evidence for the first decade of the twenty-first century is still incomplete. In a division of duties, local governments in Clark and Washoe counties have been given responsibility for local air pollution monitoring.

One additional task of the NDEP is to promote and monitor the cleanup of "brown fields," dumping sites on the edges of Nevada towns and cities left by previous generations. How can the garbage pits and piles that have accumulated over the years be rendered safe and reusable? This is only one of scores of problems left in the backyard of Nevada's foremost environmental agency.

The effectiveness of the NDEP in improving Nevada's environment will be judged in the future. The challenges become larger as the years pass, as the population of the state grows, and as land-use requirements change. This is an ongoing saga.

The Nevada Agency for Nuclear Projects

In 1983, soon after Congress passed the 1982 law designating Yucca Mountain as a possible site for the storage of high-level nuclear waste, Governor Richard Bryan issued an executive order establishing the Agency for Nuclear Projects. The 1985 session of the legislature gave this agency its endorsement and formalized assignment to monitor all federal nuclear-waste planning and proposals and to coordinate responses on behalf of the state.

Under the direction of Robert Loux, the agency has been highly effective in keeping Nevadans aware of the federal government's activities. It guides and oversees independent reviews of hydrological, geological, engineering, and other technical aspects of the project. It sponsors independent studies of the federal proposals so that the state is not totally dependent on information provided by the federal government and private nuclear power interests.

Underground Water

In chapters 3 and 4, we discussed the evolution of surface-water uses during the nineteenth and twentieth centuries and mentioned the dramatic new effort in Las Vegas to tap the underground waters of the northeastern counties. Let us return to this subject.

Virtually all Nevada surface waters are committed or overcommitted, but it appeared in the 1990s that there may be a substantial amount underground in the aquifers of the northeastern counties. The Nevada Division of Water Planning has determined that there are 14 hydrographic "regions" in Nevada, divided into 256 distinct hydrographic "basins." Many basins in rural Nevada are presumed to have substantial quantities of "uncommitted" water that might be pumped southward to the thirsty oasis. Much water now used in the rural counties of northern Nevada is committed to irrigation and livestock production—a declining business. Additional amounts sustain fish, wildlife, and plant species. There has been a sustained debate in recent decades about whether this potential source of water should be diverted southward.

The Desert Research Institute

The Desert Research Institute is nearly fifty years old as a home-grown environmental research agency. The seeds of its success were imported from distant places, and Nevada's soil proved to be receptive. The original planter of those seeds was Wendell A. Mordy, the first director, who arrived at the University of Nevada–Reno in 1958 and persuaded the state to initiate a center for scientific studies in the high desert domain. The DRI won legal endorsement in the legislature in 1959 and in the university setting because it promised to do most of its work with out-of-state grant money rather than in-state government appropriations. In an era of generous federal appropriations and private scientific expenditures, the DRI was brilliantly successful in this endeavor.

Mordy identified several possibilities for study. An atmospheric physicist, Mordy and his early colleagues focused on air quality and the possibilities of drawing water from high-level clouds that hovered above the western mountain ranges, an idea that became popular in rain-starved Nevada. The early DRI staff also directed attention to the desert biosphere, previously understudied except when it promised benefits to livestock raisers. One important early undertaking of DRI scientists was to monitor air quality at the Nevada Test Site. They held contracts when atmospheric testing occurred and after testing was moved underground to study the effects and remedies when subsurface explosions accidentally vented into the atmosphere. Its scientists also studied water quality in southern Nevada.

Although the original and primary mission of the DRI was to serve Nevada, the research of its scientists reached across the globe. In the late 1980s DRI faculties under the leadership of President

James Taranik emphasized the acquisition of data from "remote sensing," gathering information from satellites and airplanes. The DRI became an organization of international importance, serving the needs of the global community in an era of profound changes. It did research in Antarctica, in African and Australian deserts, and on ocean currents. With nearly five hundred faculty members, it normally has about a hundred research projects under way at any given time. It conducts its research through three core divisions: atmospheric, earth and ecosystem, and hydrologic.

The Sierra Club

The Sierra Club is the oldest and most respected or, in some circles, the most despised citizens' group in the public arena, depending on where one stands in the ecological debate. It is respected by environmentalists and condemned by those who rush into projects exploiting the ecosystem.

A coalition of dues-paying members with a credible voice in the dialogue in Nevada and the nation, the Sierra Club was founded in 1892 by John Muir. It has grown into a powerful advocate on behalf of the lands and waters that cannot speak for themselves. Its leaders, Gifford Pinchot and Muir, were persuasive voices for the creation of the national forests and the National Park Service. It has 275,000 members nationwide and more than 5,000 in Nevada.

The earliest and most popular goals of the Sierra Club were outings into the natural settings—mountains and deserts, in Nevada's case. The Toiyabe chapter, which embraces Nevada and much of eastern California, sponsors more than one hundred outings each year.

Active Sierra Club members moved beyond the enjoyment of the natural environment to protection of it. Advocacy before Congress and state legislatures became its broader strategy. In virtually every major environmental struggle of the past forty years, the Sierra Club has been a voice for protection of the natural heritage.

The League of Women Voters

The League of Women Voters was established in Nevada with a chapter in Reno in 1951 and a statewide organization the following year. For the first two decades its members concentrated their efforts on informing and engaging voters on electoral matters. By the late 1960s it was expanding its agenda to embrace environmental pollution.

In 1969 under the leadership of Jean Ford of Las Vegas, the league's state president, league members conducted research on the mounting evidence of air pollution in Las Vegas Valley. They obtained a federal grant under the Air Quality Act to encourage public discussion and enhance public understanding of the growing problem. Organizing conferences and generating publicity, this citizens' group gave Nevada its first significant lessons in environmental lobbying.

Jean Ford and a band of citizen lobbyists were instrumental in getting a law enacted in the 1971 legislative session that sought to bring Nevada into compliance with federal standards on air quality. In 1972 Mary Johnson and other league members produced a study titled *Land in Nevada: Planning Its Use and Misuse*. Daisy Talvitia of Las Vegas and Tina Nappe of Reno rounded out the team that became one of the most effective nonprofit voices for environmental responsibility in the history of the state.

Citizen Alert

Citizen Alert, a grassroots movement, emerged in 1975 when the idea of placing a nuclear dump at the Nevada Test Site first loomed as the state's leading environmental issue. It also called attention to the amount of land and airspace being appropriated by the Department of Defense in the last decades of the twentieth century.

A few women formed the core of Citizen Alert in the beginning. Maya Miller of Washoe Valley, who had helped finance an environmental study group, Foresta Institute, was an instrumental planner and financial supporter; Susan Orr, newly arrived from Washington, D.C., provided organizational skills; and Katharine Hale of Reno became the collector of data about the known effects of nuclear activities on children and future generations. Orr and Hale made an initial fifteen hundred–mile trip to scores of Nevada towns and ranches to draw attention to the federal proposals for making Nevada the preferred dumping site for nuclear waste. Citizen Alert grew quickly from an idea into an organization with more than a thousand members and played a leading role in opposing nuclear dumping in Nevada and militarization of Great Basin lands by federal agencies. Like the League of Women Voters, it tapped a reservoir of public concern.

Citizen Alert gradually expanded its activities to other environmental issues, including opposition to the M-X missile proposal, objections to nuclear testing, and resistance to the accelerating pattern of withdrawing public domain lands for military uses. It engaged Bob Fulkerson, a fifth-generation Nevadan, as executive director in 1984, and for ten years he energized the organization. In 1994 he shifted his talents and energy to the Progressive Leadership Alliance of Nevada, which embraced an expanded agenda of social issues.

The Progressive Leadership Alliance of Nevada

The most potent Nevada-based player in this high-stakes competition is the Progressive Leadership Alliance of Nevada. Founded in the early 1990s with twelve groups and a minuscule budget, it assumed responsibility for a broad range of local challenges, including environmental issues but also reaching into the needs of the poor and the social injustices embedded in the law. Its self-chosen mandate was based on areas of social concern neglected by the "system" but essential for human dignity and a responsible lifestyle.

The eclectic approach of PLAN to the problems facing Nevada gave energy to its member groups to coalesce around a few key issues. PLAN went to the legislature, local governments, and the public via the news media and one-on-one contacts. Ecology-oriented groups talked to Indian tribes, social workers, activists for children, women's right groups, and others about common interests and goals.

Fulkerson and Jan Gilbert, a concerned citizen from Washoe Valley, assembled an ad hoc team of social activists around the issue of the proposed nuclear dump site at Yucca Mountain and the various social issues confronting Nevada—neglect of the poor, flaws in the justice system, and failure of the state to finance basic educational and health care services at responsible levels.

By 2008 PLAN was a coalition of forty organizations working for social justice and ecological responsibility in Nevada. About half its member organizations had concerns with environmental matters. In 2002 PLAN generated the Nevada Conservation League, the state's first homegrown lobbying group in the arena.

The Nature Conservancy of Nevada

The Nature Conservancy (TNC) is a worldwide organization that for a half century has been identifying and working to protect natural biodiversity and restore the natural habitats of animals and plants threatened by human development. It is a relative newcomer to Nevada, but it has become a powerful force in the struggle to protect local and regional environments.

TNC tries to protect lands and waters largely by cooperating, serving as a mediator between competing private and governmental interests. It is best known for its purchase of land and the gifts of commitment it receives; it often works in concert with other agencies. Supported by both public and private funding, this group identifies and applies scientific methods to specific areas where possibilities for preservation of nature's resources remain and might be restored.

Although its first transaction in Nevada occurred in 1967, TNC is relatively young as a local organization, with a statewide branch emerging only in the 1990s. Long before the organization became active in Nevada, Governor Grant Sawyer in 1967 identified a site worthy of preservation in the center of the state. It contained the bones of an ichthyosaur, a sea monster that became extinct millions of years ago. Nearby was a nineteenth-century ghost town named Berlin. Because the state government had no funds to purchase the property, Governor Sawyer worked with TNC to have the land held in trust and eventually to be transferred to the state; it became the Berlin-Ichthyosaur State Park, preserving and displaying the bones of an ancient sea creature and a mining-era ghost town. This established the pattern that emerged as a major tactic for conservationists.

TNC in the early 1990s found Nevada to be a land of opportunity—just as the earliest settlers and miners and the early gamblers and military experiments had done. But in this case the state offered opportunities for *conservation* because so much of it—86 percent—was still under federal control. Much land and water had been abused, but much more could be rescued. As of 2006 TNC had identified millions of acres of endangered land and water within the state in twenty-one different areas that it hoped to protect. Some of it had been acquired, some was being purchased or held in trust until private and public funding could be arranged, some was subject to delicate negotiation, and some was on a wish list for possible future preservation.

One prime example is the McCarran Ranch property along the Truckee River, 10 miles downstream from Reno. Once the pioneering home of a prominent Irish immigrant family and the birthplace of longtime Nevada senator Pat McCarran, it was acquired by the Nature Conservancy in the early 2000s. In a section of the river that had been damaged by industrial development and well-intentioned flood-control dredging, TNC applied the skills of its scientists to restore a 5-mile portion along the river to its natural state. Birds, frogs, and native plants that had been declining are reappearing. TNC is working with public land agencies to implement this model on other parts of the river.

In southern Nevada, TNC identified the Amargosa River and Ash Meadows as one of the endangered areas that might be rescued from development. The Amargosa flows underground for most of its 125-mile course between Beatty and Death Valley, California. The oasis at Ash Meadows—the most varied in the Mojave Desert—nurtures about twenty-four endemic species not found anywhere else.

Another example of TNC's initiative is in the Red Rock Canyon–Summerlin area, west of Las Vegas. As the metropolitan area sprawled westward within the past dozen years, the organization worked with the Howard Hughes Corporation to establish a 5,000-acre buffer zone between the expanding planned community and the Red Rock region, where bighorn sheep, desert tortoises, and many varieties of wildflowers and birds thrive. This rare natural resource is within about 20 miles of the center of the city.

Other Environmental Activists

Glenn Miller and Elyssa Rosen formed the Great Basin Mine Watch (GBMW), a smaller nonprofit citizens' group based in Reno, advocating responsible care of the lands when minerals are extracted. It has been a frequent critic of the mining industry for its often loose, sometimes negligent regard for ecological issues. These citizens' voices of conscience have at times slowed the advance of the land exploiters. By comparison with their formidable adversaries, Citizen Alert and GBMW are like David challenging Goliath.

At times, the environmentalists have enjoyed small victories that energize their cause. In 2000 the Oil-Dri company planned to establish a "kitty-litter" production plant a few miles north of Reno. It proposed two large pits, with the attendant digging, hauling, and processing that go along with such an enterprise. Oil-Dri would have prospered, and it fought tenaciously before local boards and in the courts to bring the 1872 mining law into play. Environmentalists—especially the GBMW—rallied the public in opposition. The commissioners of Washoe County denied the permit, and a district court judge affirmed that decision. Kitty-litter mining was in abeyance in Nevada as of summer 2008.

Such grassroots groups have grown in numbers during the past several years in southern Nevada, and their voices are often heard in the courthouses, city halls, and legislative chambers in Carson City. They have restrained or at least delayed massive residential developments on the edge of the Red Rock Canyon National Recreation Area west of Las Vegas. Citizen protesters and environmentalists have also blocked freeway expansion and casino enlargement in the Red Rock area.

What is happening in Nevada is a microsample of what is happening to the planet. We are in the midst of a population explosion and profit-motive mode, assuming that the bottom line is money. Until recently, we have thought little about the air, land, and water around us. The struggle to protect the natural habitat from builders, promoters, and casual polluters is never finished. Commercial imperatives will continue, and so will the resistance to uncontrolled exploitation and the efforts to reclaim some of the wild places.

Conclusion

Nevada has been promoted as a "land of opportunity" since the days of the early Mormon settlers, the gold and silver rushes of early miners, and the building of the Central Pacific Railroad. It even enjoyed this label for divorce seekers of the 1920s and gambling promoters in the 1930s and later. This "land of opportunity" was in fact an impoverished needy cousin within the federal Union for most of its history, looking for handouts and hand-me-downs because it was a desert outback with few of the conventional resources enjoyed by its neighbors. Gradually, within a generation or two, those qualities that made Nevada an outcast— the vast dry spaces, exploited mines, loose social laws, and rugged individualism—made it the place of choice for military expansion, atomic experimentation, high-tech mining, resort gambling, and speculative real estate development.

One basic concept embedded in the culture of Nevada can be summarized in a tale that circulated among longtime residents of Reno several decades ago. A mayor of this pretentious little town in the 1920s tried to promote the Biggest Little City in the World for its notorious six-month (later six-week) divorces, its easy booze (during the era of Prohibition), and open gambling and prostitution (when both were illegal elsewhere in the country). He is reported to have said, "I want people to feel free to do in Reno what they don't feel free to do at home." Such an attitude operated not only when the impoverished state welcomed easy divorces and legalized gambling but also when it embraced Boulder Dam, the Hawthorne Naval Ammunition Depot, Nellis Air Force Base, and the Nevada Test Site. The same message has been heard recently in Las Vegas: "What happens in Vegas stays in Vegas."

In the 1970s this free-for-all attitude underwent a subtle change on environmental issues. In later years Nevada's citizens drew the line in the sand at the M-X missile project and seem to have drawn the line at the Yucca Mountain nuclear depository. A few Nevada leaders followed the federal government's conservation-oriented agencies in assuming that the natural resources of the state should be preserved and shared with future generations. Nonprofit groups such as Citizen Alert, the Sierra Club, PLAN, and the Nature Conservancy blew their whistles. Near the end of the first decade of the twenty-first century, the issues are still pending.

Provocative debate has flowed from this change in thinking about Nevada. Arrayed on one side are the military establishment and their financiers, urban developers, mining corporations, and many ranchers and property owners who regard the state as a perpetual place of opportunity for their activities. On the other side we find a few federal, state, and not-for-profit agencies—those who appeal for preservation of the Nevada wilderness and its quiet, unspoiled urban and rural venues—and a substantial part of the citizenry.

"Nevada is not a wasteland!" This slogan has been proclaimed from bumper stickers throughout the state, displayed most often by hard-core environmentalists. Yet for the military and for the Department of Energy, a "wasteland" is what Nevada has been for many decades. Some miners, urbanite garbage dumpers, hunters, fishermen, and picnickers have the same attitude. But we now try to recycle and occasionally to conserve water and protect the pristine parts that remain.

If we look at the panorama of uses of Nevada's land and water, the cavalcade of images is almost overwhelming. There is always more to say and do. The miners and smelters of ore came early and late, took their wealth, and left their scars and residue behind. Livestock owners used the high desert terrain for decades to fatten their cattle and ship them to distant markets with little concern for the consequences to the delicate surface of the earth. The U.S. Air Force and Navy pounded the land with untold tons of ammunition, and the U.S. Navy stored and destroyed its unwanted ordnance in the remote corners of the thinly populated desert. Then came the scientists and the federal government with their nuclear experiments, exploding their "devices" by the hundreds above, on, and below the land at the Nevada Test Site. The other agencies of the government came later, seeking places to hide their nuclear waste when they did not know what else to do with it.

How can we diagnose the wounds that recent generations have inflicted on this sprawling state and its diverse ecosystems within its recorded history? How badly has our turf been polluted, and is there anything we can do about it? This text is meant to encourage a Socratic dialogue about the environmental evolution of Nevada. Those of us who live here are entrusted with a very small plot on the planet. We have been here for a very short time, even in human terms. We may be a microcosm of the larger world in terms of what has been happening in the past century, but we are witnesses to ever larger experiments in atomic testing, nuclear waste, and creative mining than most of the rest of the developing world. One final Socratic question might be, "What is our ethical responsibility in this enterprise?"

Adams, Jonathan S. *The Future of the Wild: Radical Conservation for a Crowded World.* Boston: Beacon Press, 2006.

Ambrose, Stephen E. *Nothing Like It in the World: The Men Who Built the Transcontinental Railroad, 1863–1869.* New York: Simon and Schuster, 2000.

Balitzer, Alfred. "The Nevada State Environmental Commission." A publication of the Rose Institute of State and Local Government. Claremont, Calif.: Claremont McKenna College, 1990.

Ball, Howard. *Justice Downwind: America's Atomic Testing Program in the 1950s.* New York: Oxford University Press, 1986.

Barlett, Donald L., and James B. Steele. *Forever More: Nuclear Waste in America.* New York: W. W. Norton, 1985.

Beesley, David. *Crow's Range: An Environmental History of the Sierra Nevada.* Reno: University of Nevada Press, 2004.

Butigan, Ken. *Pilgrimage Through a Burning World: Spiritual Practice and Nonviolent Protest at the Nevada Test Site.* Albany: State University of New York Press, 2003.

Carter, Jimmy. *Keeping Faith: Memoirs of a President.* New York: Bantam Books, 1982.

Cawley, R. McGreggor. *Federal Land, Western Anger: The Sagebrush Rebellion and Environmental Politics.* Lawrence: University Press of Kansas, 1993.

City of Henderson. *Fifty Years—Henderson: An American Journey.* Henderson: City of Henderson, 2004.

Dangberg, Grace. *Conflict on the Carson: A Study of Water Litigation in Western Nevada*. Minden, Nev.: Carson Valley Historical Society, 1975.

Danner, Ruth Fenstermaker. *Gabbs Valley, Nevada: Its History and Legend*. Winnemucca: Ruth Fenstermaker Danner, 1992.

Dawson, Robert, Peter Goin, and Mary Webb. *A Doubtful River*. Reno: University of Nevada Press, 2000.

DeQuille, Dan. *The Big Bonanza*. New York: Alfred A. Knopf, 1947.

Dobbs, William T. "Southern Nevada and the Legacy of Basic Magnesium, Incorporated." *Nevada Historical Society Quarterly* 34 (Spring 1991): 273–303.

Egan, Timothy. "Las Vegas Stakes Water Claim in '90s Water War." *New York Times*, November 10, 1994, 1, 12.

Elliott, Gary E. *Senator Bible and the Politics of the New West*. Reno: University of Nevada Press, 1994.

Elliott, Russell R. *Growing Up in a Company Town: A Family in the Copper Camp of McGill, Nevada*. Reno: Nevada Historical Society, 1990.

———. *History of Nevada*. 2d ed. Lincoln: University of Nebraska Press, 1987.

———. *Servant of Power: A Political Biography of William M. Stewart*. Reno: University of Nevada Press, 1983.

Erikson, Kai. "Out of Sight, Out of Our Minds." *New York Times Magazine*, March 9, 1994, 34ff.

Fradkin, Philip L. *Fallout: An American Nuclear Tragedy*. Tucson: University of Arizona Press, 1989.

———. *A River No More: The Colorado River and the West*. Tucson: University of Arizona Press, 1984.

Francaviglia, Richard V. *Believing in Place: A Spiritual Geography of the Great Basin*. Reno: University of Nevada Press, 2003.

Gallagher, Carole. *American Ground Zero: The Secret Nuclear War*. Cambridge: MIT Press, 1993.

Glynn, Patrick. *Closing Pandora's Box: Arms Races, Arms Control, and the History of the Cold War*. New York: New Republic / Basic Books, 1992.

Goin, Peter, and C. Elizabeth Raymond. *Changing Mines in America*. Santa Fe, N.M., and Staunton, Va.: Center for American Places, 2003–2004.

Haller, Timothy George. "California-Nevada Interstate Water Compact: A Study in Controversy." Ph.D. diss., University of Nevada, 1981.

Hill, Gladwyn. "Atomic Boomtown in the Desert." *New York Times Magazine*, February 11, 1951, 14.

———. "Desert Capital of the A-Bomb." *New York Times Magazine*, February 13, 1955, 22.

Houghton, Samuel G. *A Trace of Desert Waters: The Great Basin Story.* Reno: University of Nevada Press, 1994.

Hulse, James W. "The California-Nevada Boundary: History of a Conflict." Pt. 2. *Nevada Historical Society Quarterly* 23, no. 3 (Fall 1980): 157–78.

———. *Forty Years in the Wilderness: Impressions of Nevada, 1940–1980.* Reno: University of Nevada Press, 1986.

———. "New Water Books: The Most Recent Water Warnings." *Nevada Historical Society Quarterly* 30, no. 1 (Spring 1987): 26–36.

———. *The Silver State: Nevada's History Reinterpreted.* 3d ed. Reno: University of Nevada Press, 2004.

Hundley, Norris, Jr. *The Great Thirst: Californians and Water, 1770–1990s.* Berkeley and Los Angeles: University of California Press, 1992.

———. *Water and the West: The Colorado River Compact and the Politics of Water in the American West.* Berkeley and Los Angeles: University of California Press, 1975.

Jacob, Gerald. *Site Unseen: The Politics of Siting a Nuclear Waste Repository.* Pittsburgh: University of Pittsburgh Press, 1990.

Jones, Florence Lee, and John Cahlan. *Water: A History of Las Vegas.* 2 vols. Las Vegas: Las Vegas Valley Water District, 1975.

Kluger, James R. *Turning on Water With a Shovel: The Career of Elwood Mead.* Albuquerque: University of New Mexico Press, 1992.

Knack, Martha C., and Omer C. Stewart. *As Long As the River Shall Run: An Ethnohistory of Pyramid Lake Indian Reservation.* Berkeley and Los Angeles: University of California Press, 1984.

Kuletz, Valerie L. *The Tainted Desert: Environmental and Social Ruin in the American West.* New York: Routledge, 1998.

Lambert, Darwin. *Great Basin Drama.* Niwat, Colo.: Roberts Rinehart, 1991.

Lincoln, Francis Church. *Mining Districts and Mineral Resources of Nevada.* 1923. Reprint, Las Vegas: Nevada Publications, 1982.

Loomis, David. *Combat Zoning: Military Land-Use Planning in Nevada.* Reno: University of Nevada Press, 1993.

McCracken, Robert D. *A History of Tonopah, Nevada.* Tonopah: Nye County Press, 1990.

Misrach, Richard, with Miriam Weisang Misrach. *Bravo 20: The Bombing of the American West.* Baltimore: Johns Hopkins University Press, 1990.

Moehring, Eugene P. *Resort City in the Sunbelt: Las Vegas, 1930–2000.* 2d ed. Reno: University of Nevada Press, 2000.

Moore, Roberta, and Scott Slovic. *Wild Nevada: Testimonies on Behalf of the Desert.* Reno: University of Nevada Press, 2005.

Muhn, James, and Hanson R. Stuart. *Opportunity and Challenge: The Story of the BLM.* Washington, D.C.: Department of the Interior, Bureau of Land Management, 1988.

Murchie, Archie, with R. T. King. *The Free Life of a Ranger: A Forest Service Memoir.* 2d ed. Reno: University of Nevada Oral History Program, 2002.

Nash, Gerald D. *The American West Transformed: The Impact of the Second World War.* Bloomington: Indiana University Press, 1985.

———. *World War II and the West: Reshaping the Economy.* Lincoln: University of Nebraska Press, 1990.

National Resources Defense Council. *Bulletin of the Atomic Scientists* 46 (April 1990).

Nevada, State of. *Statutes of Nevada . . . 1989, AJR 4 and AJR 6, 2263 and 2265.*

Nevada Bureau of Mines and Geology. *Geologic and Natural History Tours in the Reno Area.* Rev. ed. Nevada Bureau of Mines and Geology, Special Publication 19. Reno: University of Nevada, 2005.

———. *Geologic Tours in the Las Vegas Area.* Rev. ed. Nevada Bureau of Mines and Geology, Special Publication 16. Reno: University of Nevada, 2001.

———. *Traveling America's Loneliest Road: A Geologic and Natural History Tour Along U.S. Highway 50.* Nevada Bureau of Mines and Geology, Special Publication 26. Reno: University of Nevada, 2000.

Nevada Commission on Nuclear Projects. *Report on the State of Nevada Commission on Nuclear Projects.* Prepared for presentation to the governor and the 66th session of the Nevada legislature. Carson City: State of Nevada, September 1992.

Nevada Division of Environmental Protection. *Quality of the Environment Report.* Carson City: Nevada Division of Environmental Protection, 2001.

———. *2004 Biennial Report.* Carson City: Nevada Division of Environmental Protection, 2004.

Nevada Division of Water Planning. *Nevada State Water Plan.* Carson City: Nevada Division of Water Planning, 1999.

Parker, Robert E., and Joe R. Feagin. "Military Spending in Enterprise Cities: The Military-Industrial Complex in Houston and Las Vegas." In *The Pentagon and the Cities,* edited by Andrew Kirby. Urban Affairs Annual Reviews, vol. 40. Newbury Park, Calif.: Sage Publications, 1992.

Pearce, Fred. *When the Rivers Run Dry: Water—the Defining Crisis of the Twenty-first Century.* Boston: Beacon Press, 2006.

Pool, Peter E., ed. *The Altered Landscape.* Reno: Nevada Museum of Art / University of Nevada Press, 1999.

Reisner, Marc. *Cadillac Desert: The American West and Its Disappearing Water.* New York: Viking, 1986.

Rodden, Mimi Garat. *Images of America: Boulder City, Nevada.* Chicago: Arcadia Publishing, 2000.

Rothman, Hal K. *Neon Metropolis: How Las Vegas Started the Twenty-first Century.* New York: Routledge, 2002.

——. *Saving the Planet: The American Response to the Environment in the Twentieth Century.* Chicago: Ivan R. Dee, 2000.

Rothman, Hal K., and Char Miller, eds. *Out of the Woods: Essays in Environmental History.* Pittsburgh: University of Pittsburgh Press, 1997.

Rothstein, Linda. "Nevada Dump Ads." *Bulletin of the Atomic Scientists* 48 (May 1992): 3–4.

Rowley, William D. *Reclaiming the Arid West: The Career of Francis G. Newlands.* Bloomington: Indiana University Press, 1996.

——. *U.S. Forest Service Grazing and Rangelands.* College Station: Texas A&M University Press, 1985.

Smith, Grant H. *A History of the Comstock Lode, 1850–1920.* Bulletin 37. Reno: University of Nevada, July 1943.

Solnit, Rebecca. *Savage Dreams: A Journey Into the Hidden Wars of the American West.* 1994. Reprint, Berkeley and Los Angeles: University of California Press, 1999.

Starrs, Paul F. *Let the Cowboy Ride: Cattle Ranching in the American West.* Baltimore: Johns Hopkins University Press, 1998.

Stevens, Joseph E. *Hoover Dam: An American Adventure.* Norman: University of Oklahoma Press, 1988.

Strong, Douglas H. *Tahoe: An Environmental History.* Lincoln: University of Nebraska Press, 1984.

——. *Tahoe: From Timber Barons to Ecologists.* Lincoln: University of Nebraska Press, 1999.

Sudol, Stan. "The Republic of Mining." *Fraser Report* (March 3, 2008).

Titus, A. Costandina. *Bombs in the Backyard: Atomic Testing and American Politics.* 2d ed. Reno: University of Nevada Press, 2001.

Townley, John M. *Alfalfa Country: Nevada Land, Water, and Politics in the Nineteenth Century.* Reno: University of Nevada Agricultural Experiment Station, 1981.

——. *Turn This Water Into Gold: The Story of the Newlands Project.* Reno: Nevada Historical Society, 1977.

U.S. Bureau of Land Management. *The Great Basin: Healing the Land.* Washington, D.C.: Department of the Interior, Bureau of Land Management, 2000.

U.S. Department of Energy. Nevada Operations Office. *United States Nuclear Tests: July 1945 Through September 1992.* DOE/NV-209. N.p.: U.S. Department of Energy, 1994.

U.S. Department of Energy. Office of Civilian Radioactive Waste Management. *Final Supplemental Environmental Impact Statement for a Geologic Repository for the Disposal of Spent Nuclear Fuel and High-Level Radioactive Waste at Yucca Mountain, Nye County, Nevada.* N.p.: U.S. Department of Energy, June 2008.

———. *Nevada Rail Transportation Corridor: DOE EI-0250F-S2D and Draft Environmental Impact Statement for a Rail Alignment for the Construction and Operation of a Railroad in Nevada to a Geologic Repository at Yucca Mountain, Nevada.* N.p.: U.S. Department of Energy, June 2008.

U.S. Department of Energy. Office of Environmental Management. "Central Nevada Test Area." In *A Report to the Congress on Long-Term Stewardship.* Vol. 2, *Site Summaries.* N.p.: U.S. Department of Energy, January 2001.

U.S. Statutes at Large. 96 Stat. 2201-2263; 101 Stat. 1330 227232.

Wheeler, Session S. *The Desert Lake: The Story of Nevada's Pyramid Lake.* Caldwell, Ida.: Caxton Printers, 1969.

Worster, Donald. *Rivers of Empire: Water, Aridity, and the Growth of the American West.* New York: Pantheon Books, 1985.

Wuerthner, George, and Mollie Matteson, eds. *Welfare Ranching: The Subsidized Destruction of the American West.* Washington, D.C.: Island Press, 2002.

Young, James A., and B. Abbott Sparks. *Cattle in the Cold Desert.* 1985. Reprint, Reno: University of Nevada Press, 2002.

Zanjani, Sally. *Sarah Winnemucca.* Lincoln: University of Nebraska Press, 2001.

Page numbers in italics refer to maps, and page number *70* in italics refers to the photographic plates (pl.) following page 70.

lumber mills, 49, 70 pls. 3–4
Luning, 25

magnesium industry, 23–26, 24, 27
Matteson, Mollie, 8
McCarran, Pat, 26, 118
McCarran International Airport, 55,
  69–70, 70 pl. 11
McCarran Ranch property, conservation
  project at, 118
McGill, 20–22
McGill, William, 20
Mead, Lake: aerial view of, 70 pl. 10;
  perchlorate in, 66; water level drop in,
  60; water pumped from, 26, 58, 65,
  66, 69
mercury: atmospheric, 31, 32–33; in earth,
  31; water contamination from, 17,
  37–38, 70 pl. 8
Mesquite, 64
military operations: attitudes on, 71, 73,
  79–80; classified, 74, 100; in Cold
  War era, 81; debris from, 70 pl. 12;
  Defense Department, 93, 96, 115; in
  desert, 81, 82; economic aspects of,
  73; environmental impact of, 73, 74,
  75–76, 77; in Great Basin, 116; growth
  of, 72, 121; ordnance, 74, 123; wasteland
  created by, 122. See also ammunition
Miller, Bob, 94
Miller, Glenn, 119
Miller, Maya, 115–16
Minden, 107
minerals, nonfuel, 30, 65–66
mining industry: air pollution generated
  by, 21, 27, 32–33; arrival of, 1;
  attitudes toward, 33, 34; critics of, 30,
  119; dormant period of, 18–19, 29;
  employment in, 30; environmental
  impact of, 11, 30–32, 34, 37–38, 66,
  123; federal monitoring of, 105; forests
  impacted by, 16–17, 37, 40; funding
  for, 89; kitty-litter mining, 119–20;
  land acquisition by, 2; Nevada State
  Environmental Commission and,
  110; tailings, 70 pl. 5; technology,
  15–16, 19–23, 29, 31–32, 37, 121; water
  pollution, role in, 52–53, 65; water
  pumping by, 31, 52–53
mining law, of 1872, 18–19

mining towns, 13, 22, 23–28
Misrach, Richard, and Myriam Weisang,
  75–76
Mohave, Lake. See Lake Mohave
Mono Lake, 67
Mormons, 36, 64, 79
Mormon Station. See Genoa
mountain fires, 14
Mount Davidson, 16, 38
Muir, John, 109, 114
mustard gas contamination, 77
m-x missile, 78–80, 81, 108, 116, 122

National Academy of Sciences, 94
National Environmental Policy Act (nepa),
  107–8
national parks, dangers to, 10, 109
National Park Service, 114
National Register of Historic Places, 88
Native Americans: agriculture and, 48,
  51; displacement of, 1; environmental
  group and, 117; nuclear testing opposed
  by, 85; rights of, advocates for, 50;
  tribal lands of, 47, 103
native grasses, 6, 8
natural habitats, restoring, 117
Nature Conservancy of Nevada, 117–19, 122
Naval Ammunition Depot (nad)
  (Hawthorne), 51, 76–77, 122
Nellis Air Force Base, 72–74, 81, 97, 122
Nevada Agency for Nuclear Projects, 92, 112
Nevada Conservation League, 117
Nevada Department of Environmental
  Protection (ndep), 23, 36
Nevada Division of Environmental
  Protection, 110–11
Nevada Division of Water Planning, 52, 112
Nevada Mining Association (nma), 30, 32
Nevada State Environmental Commission,
  109–10
Nevada Test Site: air quality at, 113; atomic
  bomb explosion at, 70 pl. 13; attitudes
  concerning, 122; contamination
  produced by, 86; establishment of, 81;
  as environmental issue, 115; location
  of, 78; as nuclear waste site, 81; nuclear
  waste sites compared to, 95, 96;
  operations at, 82–84, 123; in post–Cold
  War era, 87–88; protest demonstrations
  at, 70 pl. 14, 85; radioactive wastes